Behavioral Relaxation Training and Assessment

Second Edition

Behavioral Relaxation Training and Assessment

Second Edition

Roger Poppen

SAGE Publications
International Educational and Professional Publisher
Thousand Oaks London New Delhi

For information:

SAGE Publications, Inc.
2455 Teller Road
Thousand Oaks, California 91320
E-mail: order@sagepub.com

SAGE Publications Ltd.
6 Bonhill Street
London EC2A 4PU
United Kingdom

SAGE Publications India Pvt. Ltd.
M-32 Market
Greater Kailash I
New Delhi 110 048 India

Printed in the United States of America

Library of Congress Cataloging-in-Publication Data

Poppen, Roger.
    Behavioral relaxation training and assessment / by Roger Poppen. —
2nd ed.
        p.   cm.
    Includes bibliographical references and index.
    ISBN 0-7619-1200-2 (hardcover: alk. paper). — ISBN 0-7619-1201-0
(pbk.: alk. paper)
    1. Relaxation—Study and teaching—Philosophy. 2. Relaxation—
Methodology. 3. Behaviorism (Psychology). I. Title.
    BF637.R45P66 1998
    158'.9—dc21   97-45278

This book is printed on acid-free paper.

98 99 00 01 02 03 10 9 8 7 6 5 4 3 2 1

Acquiring Editor:	Jim Nageotte
Editorial Assistant:	Fiona Lyon
Production Editor:	Astrid Virding
Production Assistant:	Denise Santoyo
Book Designer/Typesetter:	Janelle LeMaster
Cover Designer:	Candice Harman
Print Buyer:	Anna Chin

Contents

Acknowledgments

A ppreciation is expressed to LiMing Poppen for the illustrations of the relaxed postures and to Maria DePerczel for posing. Many students contributed to the development and application of Behavioral Relaxation Training whose efforts are not directly cited in this book. The following were gratefully acknowledged in the first edition: Laura Davis, Paul Erlandson, Edward Jiang, Fred Ribet, David Rush, David Sievert, and David Wheeler. To that list, I would like to add the following: Tim Cripps, Jennifer Eliason, Rosalia Fulia, Carrie Peacock, Jon Kuh, Clayton Rathbun, Rick Reiling, Leslie Trautman, and Jianhong Wu.

To Tamara, Lisa,
Max, and Serena

1

A Behavioral Analysis
of Relaxation

R elaxation training, in its many guises, is a major component in
behaviorally based interventions for anxiety, stress, and pain
disorders (Borkovec & Costello, 1993; Lehrer, Carr, Sargunaraj, &
Woolfolk, 1994; National Institutes of Health Technology Assessment Panel, 1996). Its ubiquity has led some to call it the "aspirin" of
behavioral medicine (Russo, Bird, & Masek, 1980). Hundreds of
published articles, ranging from clinical case reports to multifactorial
controlled group designs, attest to the effectiveness of relaxation
training, or treatment "packages" containing relaxation, in the treatment of these disorders. Yet, for all its popularity in application, the
phenomenon of relaxation itself has received relatively little attention. Training often is employed in a "cookbook" fashion with only
vague or speculative notions about how or why it may be effective.

1

Researchers and practitioners seldom measure what their trainees are doing and how it is related to treatment outcome (Ludwick-Rosenthal & Neufeld, 1988; Luiselli, Marholin, D. Steinman, & W. Steinman, 1979). Relaxation training procedures proliferate, with this book presenting yet another one. But without a rational and empirical basis, the trainer has little guidance in selecting from the various techniques and in evaluating his or her choice. One purpose of this book is to provide such guidance.

This first chapter presents an overview of current theories of relaxation and methods of training. It maintains a behavioral orientation, emphasizing the physical and social environment in which training takes place and the behavior of the trainee. The goal is to provide a common framework by which to organize the diversity of procedures and behaviors that control the professional use of the term "relaxation." This chapter also provides the foundation for the behavioral assessment and training procedures described in subsequent chapters.

THEORIES OF RELAXATION

Relaxation theories provide conceptual systems that describe the multitude of relaxation procedures and the even more varied effects of engaging in those procedures. Some theorists propose that relaxation is a single state or condition, whereas others propose that there are two or even more types or components of relaxation. These are discussed here as unitary, dualistic, and multimodal theories.

Unitary Theories

Pride of place goes to Edmund Jacobson, who may be called the father of relaxation (Jacobson, 1929/1938). He developed progressive relaxation, which is the basis of the most common training procedures employed in behavior therapy and behavioral medicine. He also developed electromyographic (EMG) methods of assessment. He championed the use of relaxation for a diverse range of maladies and provided case reports of its effectiveness.

Muscular Theory

Jacobson (1929/1938) defined relaxation as the quiescence of skeletal muscle activity, as measured peripherally by the EMG. At the neurological level, he proposed a diminished motoneuron output and a reduced proprioceptive input, citing as evidence his research on the reduced magnitude and increased latency of spinal motor reflexes when a person is relaxed. He further proposed that, as a result of reduced afferent and efferent activity in the skeletal-motor system, autonomic and cortical arousal is decreased, citing anatomical and physiological data supporting a correlation between these systems. Thus, neuromuscular relaxation could have salutory effects on diverse physiological, "neurotic," and "emotional" disorders that involve cortical and autonomic structures. Later research on animals verified that posterior hypothalamic and sympathetic arousal is directly related to muscular proprioceptive activity (Gellhorn & Loofbourrow, 1963).

Autonomic Theory

Later writers emphasized the autonomic rather than the muscular aspects of relaxation. The involvement of autonomically innervated visceral structures in emotional and stress disorders, as well as the reciprocal relationship between the sympathetic and parasympathetic branches of the autonomic nervous system, has provided an easily understood mechanism of relaxation.

Joseph Wolpe, a major founder of the discipline of behavior therapy, revived the dormant procedure of Jacobson (Poppen, 1995). His adaptation of progressive relaxation training was a central feature of systematic desensitization, a clinical procedure that opened the door to behavioral treatments of anxiety disorders. Wolpe (1958) conceived of relaxation as the parasympathetic antithesis of sympathetically mediated anxiety. According to this view, the parasympathetic state of relaxation "reciprocally inhibited" the sympathetic state of anxiety. Later theories of relaxation and anxiety have grown more complex, but the idea of relaxation as an antidote to problematic arousal remains a central feature of most treatment programs.

Herbert Benson, an important figure in the development of behavioral medicine, also presented a parasympathetic theory of relaxation, emphasizing its effects on various medical conditions (Benson, 1975; Benson, Beary, & Carol, 1974; Wallace, Benson, & Wilson, 1971). Benson employed meditation rather than progressive relaxation, but he proposed that the common denominator of all techniques was the "relaxation response" of parasympathetic dominance. According to this view, relaxation represents a shift in autonomic activity away from sympathetic arousal toward parasympathetic control. Thus, a relaxed state is characterized by any of a number of parasympathetically mediated visceral activities such as decreased heart rate, respiratory rate, blood pressure, and oxygen consumption. One also would expect relaxation to inhibit visceral activities mediated solely by the sympathetic system, resulting in increased peripheral vasodilation and skin resistance.

Three problems exist with the parasympathetic theory—one conceptual, one empirical, and one practical.

Conceptually, it is not clear which visceral systems should show parasympathetic dominance during relaxation. A widely held view is that relaxation is a trophotropic (or energy-restorative) response, providing homeostatic balance for the ergotropic fight-or-flight response (Benson et al., 1974; Gellhorn & Loofbourrow, 1963; Hess, 1957; Stoyva, 1977). One might suppose that a unitary trophotropic system also would include digestive secretions, gastric motility, and sexual tumescence. Although restorative in function, these parasympathetic actions usually are not considered to be components of relaxation. A related problem is that parasympathetic activity is not universally benign; vasodilation in migraine, bronchial constriction in asthma, and acid secretion in gastric ulcer are but a few examples of problematic parasympathetic activities. According to autonomic theory, one might expect such conditions to be exacerbated by relaxation. But instead, relaxation methods often are found to be useful in treatment programs for these disorders.

One might seek to avoid this conceptual problem by empirically defining relaxation as those parasympathetic activities that change as a result of relaxation training. However, despite decades of research, there is no set of parasympathetic responses that is consistently related to all relaxation training procedures for all trainees or even to a particular procedure for persons in a particular diagnostic category (Hillenberg & Collins, 1982; Holmes, 1984; Qualls & Sheehan, 1981). Failure to find an expected change in a particular autonomic system may be due to an inappropriate definition of relaxation, an inadequate training procedure, or an idiosyncratic trainee. This is not to deny that relaxation procedures result in autonomic changes or that these changes may be beneficial to many individuals. The empirical problem is just that we do not yet know which training variables in combination with which individual variables result in what autonomic outcomes. A blanket parasympathetic theory provides no guidance in answering these questions.

Finally, a practical problem with the parasympathetic theory is that measures of autonomic activity are cumbersome, expensive, intrusive, and reactive to a variety of variables unrelated to relaxation. Because of these problems, autonomic assessment of relaxation usually is ignored except in special research settings. Consequently, a parasympathetic conceptualization of relaxation does not provide the clinician with a way in which to determine how well the trainee is learning the skill of relaxation.

Summary

Among the unitary theories, Jacobson (1929/1938) advocated a muscular basis for relaxation, whereas Wolpe (1958), Benson (Benson, 1975; Benson, Beary, & Carol, 1974; Wallace, Benson, & Wilson, 1971) and other noted investigators have emphasized parasympathetic activity. It is generally accepted that muscle tension and sympathetic activity are directly related. Although a de facto consensus exists in terms of frequently employed measures of relaxation (e.g., frontalis EMG, heart rate, blood pressure, electrodermal (EDR) activity, skin temperature, oxygen uptake), no consistent evidence for the necessity or sufficiency of these measures exists. In addition, as described in subsequent sections, many investigators believe that relaxation involves more than a pattern of physiological activity, whatever those patterns may prove to be.

On the training side of the equation, Jacobson (1929/1938) and Wolpe (1958) employed muscular tense-release exercises, whereas Benson (Benson, 1975; Benson, Beary, & Carol, 1974; Wallace, Benson, & Wilson, 1971) employed a secular form of meditation. Benson proposed a unitary theory of relaxation training, suggesting that all training procedures are comprised of the same basic ingredients. This notion is discussed later.

Dualistic Theory

The contemporary version of the ancient separation of human experience into "mind" and "body" is the distinction between "cognitive" and "somatic." Many investigators have applied these concepts to relaxation, suggesting that they describe distinct aspects of relaxation and associated training methods (Davidson & Schwartz, 1976; Heide & Borkovec, 1983; Lehrer, Woolfolk, Rooney, McCann, & Carrington, 1983). As did Wolpe (1958), proponents of this view often discuss relaxation in the context of its antithesis, anxiety, which also is described as having both cognitive and somatic components (Borkovec & Costello, 1993; Norton & Johnson, 1983; Sapp, 1996).

Somatic Relaxation

According to dualistic theory, somatic relaxation involves the muscular, visceral, or neurological mechanisms described by unitary theories. In addition to, or often in place of, direct measures of physiological activity, investigators employ self-report ratings, such as the Cognitive-Somatic Anxiety Questionnaire (Schwartz, Davidson, & Goleman, 1978) and the Test Anxiety Inventory (Spielberger, 1983), concerning the occurrence of various physical symptoms. Like the unitary theorists, dualists do not provide specification as to which somatic activities are necessary or sufficient for relaxation. Nor have they demonstrated a clear-cut relationship between self-report ratings and actual physiological measures.

Cognitive Relaxation

This aspect of relaxation consists of a subjective experience of calmness. It often is measured in negative terms on self-report scales as low ratings of worry, disturbing thoughts, or other undesirable mental states. Smith (1989) proposed three cognitive processes necessary for relaxation: "focusing," "passivity," and "receptivity." Although Davidson and Schwartz (1976) discussed the use of EDR and electroencephalographic measures of cognitive activity, the usual criterion for subjective experience is the individual's report of it. As such, reports are taken at face value and validation is considered only in terms of intercorrelations among various self-report scales.

Relaxation Training

Dualistic theorists have not suggested any new procedures for teaching relaxation but have separated existing ones into cognitive and somatic categories based on the behavior of the trainee and hypotheses about the mechanisms involved. For example, variations of progressive relaxation and physical exercise are categorized as "somatic" methods, whereas meditation, hypnosis, and imagery methods are categorized as "cognitive" (Borkovec & Costello, 1993; Cauthen & Prymak, 1977; Lehrer et al., 1983; Norton & Johnson, 1983; Sapp, 1996; Schwartz et al., 1978). Research has taken the form of comparing groups of persons trained in somatic methods to groups trained in cognitive methods on a variety of physiological and self-report measures. One goal of such research has been to show a greater effect of cognitive training on cognitive measures and of somatic training on somatic measures. Another goal has been to show that people with relatively higher cognitive anxiety respond better to cognitive training and that those with higher somatic anxiety respond better to somatic training. The most common findings have been that both somatic and cognitive relaxation training procedures produce changes in a therapeutic direction on both self-report and physiological measures. This is interpreted as supporting a "generalized relaxation response" (Lehrer et al., 1983; Schwartz et al., 1978). Some predicted relationships have been found between cognitive or somatic training and cognitive or somatic measures, although these are not consistent across measures or studies (Norton & Johnson, 1983; Sapp, 1996; Schwartz et al., 1978). Schwartz et al. (1978) suggested that smaller specific effects related to particular techniques may be superimposed on the more general relaxation response.

Going beyond the notion of enhanced benefit when there is a match between the individual's predominant type of anxiety and the type of relaxation training, some researchers have proposed that a mismatch contributes to the phenomenon of "relaxation-induced anxiety" (RIA), whereby people experience adverse reactions during relaxation training. Some studies have found small but statistically significant relationships in the predicted direction between some measures of cognitive and somatic personality predispositions and outcome measures indicative of RIA (Heide & Borkovec, 1983; Norton & Johnson, 1983; Norton, Rhodes, Hauch, & Kaprowy, 1985).

Other researchers have found RIA to be a much more complicated phenomenon that cannot be described simply as due to cognitively anxious people receiving somatic training and vice versa (Braith, McCullough, & Bush, 1988; Heide & Borkovec, 1984; Ley, 1988; Wells, 1990).

Summary

Dualistic theory proposes that just as anxiety may be more or less mental or physical, relaxation and its various training methods are similarly divided. One goal of this approach is to provide a rationale for the observation that not all training procedures work equally well for all individuals. The categorization of disorders and training procedures along cognitive and somatic dimensions provides a basis for selecting among the various methods and predicting the most efficacious outcome. Davidson and Schwartz (1976) proposed that somatic relaxation methods have greater effects on somatic anxiety, whereas cognitive methods are better for cognitive anxiety. In a similar vein, Heide and Borkovec (1983) suggested that the phenomenon of RIA is related to the inappropriate application of a somatic training method with a person having cognitive anxiety and vice versa.

Unfortunately, there are many difficulties in defining and measuring somatic and cognitive states. Somatic relaxation and arousal, as discussed in the previous section on unitary theories, is considered to result from activity in various autonomically innervated organs and/or skeletal-muscle systems. It is measured by physiological recording or self-report of bodily symptoms. These measures are highly idiosyncratic across individuals and often show little correspondence between self-report and physiological channels. As for cognitive relaxation and arousal, it is not clear whether these states exist in some nonphysical mental realm or reflect activity in unspecified central nervous system structures. Cognitive states usually are measured by self-report inventories. These show some consistency across time, as in the Trait Anxiety Inventory (Spielberger, 1983), and are related to other measures such as academic test performance (Sapp, 1996) and psychiatric diagnosis (Borkovec & Costello, 1993). However, given the relatively large effects of either somatic or cognitive relaxation training methods on both cognitive and somatic measures, the statistical relations among more specific measures that occasionally do emerge so far have added little to our ability to predict who will benefit most from which relaxation method.

Three-Dimensional Theories

These theories propose that there are at least three categories of relaxation. They can be viewed as expansions or modifications of the dualistic model, adding new dimensions or unfolding existing ones.

Davidson and Schwartz (1976) embellished their basic dualistic theory by adding a third modality, termed "attentional," that referred to the restriction and opening up of "awareness." Cutting across these 3 broad categories, they also proposed a dimension of cortical hemispheric specialization (right-brain and left-brain activation) and an "active-passive" dimension. Thus, their 3 basic categories (cognitive/somatic/attentional) were multiplied by 2 other two-factor dimensions (right-brain/left-brain and active-passive), resulting in 12 possible categories of relaxation. Additional dimensions, such as internally generated or externally occurring stimuli, further complicate the picture.

The primary purpose of a categorization scheme is to clarify, and in this respect the Davidson and Schwartz (1976) system is not successful. First, it is not clear how "attention" or "awareness" is distinct from "cognition" in dualistic theory rather than being a subset of cognitive processes. This points up the difficulty in defining cognitive states. Second, "hemispheric specialization" appears to be a neurological metaphor for certain types of behavior. The activity of the brain is not directly observed but rather inferred from behavior. Greater clarity could be achieved by describing the behavior and the conditions under which it occurs rather than the hypothetical activity of neural structures or psychological states. Finally, the "activity" dimension is included to account for the fact that in some instances physical activity, such as jogging or dance, may be relaxing. But it is not clear whether these are to be regarded as relaxation techniques or simply that one can feel relaxed (or not) while engaging in any number of activities, from walking to skydiving.

A positive contribution of the Davidson and Schwartz (1976) theory is the idea that relaxation consists of several classes of events and that various training methods emphasize different aspects of relaxation. Also inherent in this system is the idea that various disorders involve maladaptive activity in a particular response mode and that a relaxation procedure that emphasizes that mode would be therapeutic. Although Davidson and Schwartz were primarily concerned with anxiety, this notion can be expanded to include other maladies.

Lehrer et al. (1994) suggested three categories of relaxation training methods based on the main targets or outcomes of training: "muscular," "autonomic," and "cognitive." This also can be regarded as an expansion of the dualistic approach, splitting the "somatic" mode into muscular and autonomic components. These investigators reviewed a large number of basic and clinical research studies that compared two or more "stress management" techniques on a variety of outcome measures, tallying the number of reports that found Technique X superior to Technique Y versus the number that found Technique Y equal or superior to Technique X. They discussed the limitations of their tallying method of comparing one study to another, such as ignoring magnitude of effects and methodological shortcomings, but concluded that the examination of consistency of effects over a large number of studies provided valuable insight into the mechanism of relaxation.

Lehrer et al. (1994) found that, in very general terms, one gets what one trains for; muscular techniques produced greater effects on muscular measures and symptoms, autonomic techniques had greater effects on autonomic measures and symptoms, and cognitive techniques had greater effects on cognitive measures and symptoms. They recognized that a "general relaxation effect" may obscure the more specific effect of a technique and that techniques often are not pure exemplars of a category. For example, progressive relaxation, a "muscular" technique, has more "cognitive" elements than does EMG biofeedback, another muscular procedure, making the latter more effective in producing EMG changes. In addition, some anomalies were found (as in meditation, a "cognitive" procedure) that appeared to have stronger autonomic effects than did several autonomic procedures such as thermal biofeedback. The basis for mixtures of categories within a technique, or the cross-category effects of various techniques, was not addressed by these authors. Another three-category approach was taken by Schilling and Poppen (1983). They applied Lang's (1968) conceptualization of anxiety measurement to relaxation. Lang had described the operational definition of fear as involving three types of measurements corresponding to three response systems: "behavioral," "verbal," and "physiological." In a fearsome situation, an anxious person may exhibit overt action (avoidance), verbal self-report (fear rating), and physiological arousal (increased heart rate or muscle tension). To some extent, this system modifies dualistic theory, restricting "cognition" to verbal behavior and splitting the "somatic" component into parts observed with and without electronic equipment. Schilling and Poppen noted that relaxation could be observed and measured just as anxiety is in terms of the individual's overt behavior, verbal report, and physiological activity.

This approach has certain limitations. First, operational definitions emphasize the behavior of the observer more than that of the trainee. The three categories refer to whether the trainer is observing the trainee's overt actions, verbal self-reports, or electronic instruments attached to the trainee. Second, this approach ignores the functional aspects of behavior. For example, a trainee's verbal self-report of relaxation may be related to a feeling of calmness, a desire to please the trainer, or a need to escape an unpleasant situation. Third, limiting the use of the term "behavior" to overt actions implies that verbal and physiological activities are something else. To the behavior analyst, all observable activity is "behavior" including verbal report and physiological responses. Fourth, identifying "cognition" as "verbal" seems to omit many other behaviors that it seems to encompass, however vaguely.

On the positive side, this approach suggested that various "states," such as emotions and relaxation, can be regarded as complex behaviors made up of covarying components. The particular state depends on the particular mix of components. In addition, as suggested by other multidimensional approaches, various relaxation training procedures can be seen as emphasizing particular modes of behavior. This theory served as one of the antecedents for a four-dimensional approach that seeks to address the limitations just described.

Table 1.1:   Four Modalities With Examples of Relaxed Behavior

Behavior Modality	Function	Relaxation Examples	
Motoric	Manipulates physical environment	Overt:	Relaxed postures
		Covert:	Low muscle tension
Verbal	Manipulates social environment	Overt:	Rating scale
		Covert:	Silent mantra
Visceral	Maintains internal environment	Overt:	Diaphragmatic breathing
		Covert:	Slow heart rate
Observational	Seeks and differentiates stimuli	Overt:	Closed eyes
		Covert:	Pleasant imagery

Four-Modality Theory

Poppen (1988, 1989) presented a behavioral taxonomy for the analysis of complex behavior that can be applied to relaxation. This system adheres to the level of observable behavior and does not propose explanations in mental, chemical, or neurological realms. According to this theory, complex behavior, including relaxation, involves responding in four behavioral domains. Various relaxation techniques emphasize one or another of these modes and downplay or ignore others. This behavioral taxonomy delineates all the domains of behavior in which relaxation can occur, providing a framework for the analysis of interactions between the various aspects of relaxation behavior as well as for the analysis of various training methods.

As shown in Table 1.1, there are four general categories of behavior termed "motoric," "verbal," "visceral," and "observational." Behavior in each domain may be further described according to both its functional and structural properties. Although recognizing that neurophysiological and biochemical structures underlie behavior, this approach emphasizes its functional properties.

Each of these modes of behavior is further divided into two aspects: "overt behavior" (which can be publicly observed) and "covert behavior" (which is observable only to the individual engaging in the behavior). Overt behavior can, in principle, be observed by another person—seen, heard, or palpated. Covert behavior can only be observed—felt or sensed as well as seen or heard—by an audience of one, the behaving person (Skinner, 1953). Physiological instruments may be employed to enhance observation by either party of any mode of behavior, but "physiology" is not itself a category of behavior. Relaxation may be described as behavior occurring in each of these four modalities.

Motoric Behavior

As the name implies, motoric behavior functions to move one's body, or parts of it, and to manipulate the physical environment. Structurally, it involves the skeletal-muscle system. Motoric behavior is controlled by the contingencies of physical and social reinforcement including imitative and instructional control.

Relaxed motoric behavior is characterized by low levels of activity in muscle groups not required for movement or postural maintenance. Low levels of muscle activity result in overt relaxed postures, which are described more completely in Chapters 2 and 3. Muscle tension may be covertly observed by the trainee. Jacobson invented EMG to provide an overt measure of covert muscle tension although, as Skinner (1969) noted, "the scales read by the scientist are not the private events themselves" (p. 226).

Relaxed motoric behavior also may occur when the person engages in movement; relaxation does not require inactivity. Relaxed active motoric behavior is smooth, rhythmic, and coordinated. Unrelaxed motoric behavior involves unnecessary tension and jerky, abrupt, or uncoordinated movements. Active motor relaxation may be enhanced by training in Tai Chi (Wu & Poppen, 1996) or the Alexander Technique (Brennan, 1996), procedures that have received little experimental attention.

Verbal Behavior

This category of behavior functions to mediate social reinforcement (Skinner, 1957). It is the primary means of manipulating, and being manipulated by, one's social environment. Structurally, the human vocal system is dedicated to verbal behavior, whereas motoric (e.g., gesturing) and observational (e.g., listening) modalities also are intimately involved in the service of verbal behavior. Facial expressions are a primitive type of verbal behavior. Verbal behavior is controlled by social reinforcement contingencies, with instructional and imitative variables playing a major role.

There are many verbal aspects of relaxation. Overt relaxed verbal behavior is characterized by reports of calm and well-being. Such statements may be taken as public descriptions of private events, although the social contingencies influencing self-reports must be considered. Covert verbal behavior includes listening to and silently repeating the trainer's instructions. In settings requiring vocal interaction, the content of relaxed verbal behavior is relevant to the topic, and noncontent aspects (e.g., pitch, prosody) may be characterized as calm. Unrelaxed verbal behavior includes negative self-reports, tangential content, and irregular delivery.

Visceral Behavior

Behavior in this modality functions to maintain the internal environment of the individual. Structurally, it involves smooth and cardiac muscle and the glandular systems innervated by the autonomic nervous system. Visceral behavior is controlled by reflex and respondent conditioning principles. Some visceral activity may be controlled by its effect on the environment, as when a child cries to obtain a reward, but the mediation of other behavior modalities cannot be ruled out (Miller, 1978).

An example of overt visceral behavior characteristic of relaxation is slow and regular breathing. In settings requiring exertion, relaxed breathing is more rapid but is deep and rhythmic. Covert relaxed visceral behavior includes slow and regular heartbeat, lowered blood pressure, and peripheral vasodilation. People may be able to observe these covert responses in themselves, but special instruments usually are required for accurate measurement. Unrelaxed visceral behavior involves the fight-or-flight activation of various glands and smooth muscles, although the particular pattern of arousal depends on the situation and the individual. Thus, blushing, blanching, crying, and (as described in television antiperspirant commercials) axial sweating are commonly regarded as unrelaxed visceral behavior.

Observational Behavior

Behavior in this modality functions to seek and select discriminative stimuli. Structurally, it involves the sensory systems, often in conjunction with motoric behavior, as when one turns one's head to look at or listen to the source of stimulation. Observational behavior is controlled by operant, instructional, and respondent principles.

Relaxed overt observational behavior is characterized by steadily attending to repetitive, low-intensity stimuli such as the trainer's voice or a biofeedback signal. This behavior is enhanced by restricting external distracting stimulation. Trainees often are instructed to engage in covert observational behavior, attending to interoceptive stimuli and engaging in imagery—"seeing in the absence of the thing seen" as Skinner (1974) trenchantly described it. Covert observational behavior is measured primarily by self-report and is difficult to verify because there is no access to the events being observed. In settings requiring action, relaxed observational behavior involves systematically seeking and attending to task-relevant cues.

Summary

These four categories of behavior might be regarded as an expansion of dualistic theory, dividing the "somatic" category into motoric and visceral classes (similar to the "muscular" and "autonomic" categories of Lehrer et al., 1994) and the "cognitive" category into verbal and observational classes (the latter similar to the "attentional" category of Davidson & Schwartz, 1976). However, the emphasis of four-modality theory is on behavior, as well as the environmental factors that control behavior, rather than on physiological or psychological mechanisms. Like other multimodal theories, the implication is that targeting an adaptive response as an alternative to a problematic one in a particular domain will have the most beneficial effect. Four-modality theory allows greater specificity than does the "somatic" or "cognitive" category. It also is apparent that these modalities are interdependent, and the relationships among responses within and among the four domains await empirical investigation. It is obvious that not all relaxed behaviors in all modalities occur in all settings. We use the term "relaxed" to describe ourselves or others when we observe particular constellations of behavior in particular settings, but the necessary and sufficient conditions controlling the use of that term remain to be specified.

The Response Class of Relaxation

Relaxation may be regarded as a response class involving behavior in all four domains. A response class is made up of members that covary; the occurrence of one behavior is associated with the increased likelihood of occurrence of other behaviors. Covariation occurs both within a modality (e.g., decreasing muscle tension in the jaw also may decrease tension around the eyes and forehead) and across modalities (e.g., decreased muscle tension in the face may be related to the verbal statement, "I feel calm"). Such covariation is responsible for the generalized relaxation effect of many specific techniques.

The nature and extent of such interbehavioral controls are not well understood and await further research. Some members of a response class may be genetically linked, as proposed by the autonomic theory discussed previously, in which diminished muscle tension influences visceral activity. Other links result from ontogenic experience, as when listening to the verbal description of a peaceful scene results in visual imagery. The directionality of influence also is at issue; for example, peripheral vasodilation may serve as the antecedent for the statement "My hands are warm," but will repeating "My hands are warm" produce vasodilation?

Viewing relaxation as a response class makes explicit the assumptions of various theories and training procedures. It provides a framework for answering questions about what behaviors occur in what individuals in what settings and with what outcomes. The following section looks at several of the most popular training procedures in terms of this behavioral taxonomy.

RELAXATION TRAINING METHODS

The taxonomy presented in the previous section provides a means of describing relaxation in common terms regardless of the particular training procedure. This section examines the antecedents and behaviors involved in several popular training techniques, looking at the similarities and differences. The clinical consequences of relaxation training in each of the four behavior modalities are discussed in Chapter 5.

Features Common to All Training Procedures

Benson's Four Factors

There are many features common to an array of relaxation training procedures. Benson, in keeping with his unitary theory, proposed that there are four components common to all methods, implying that these are necessary and sufficient for relaxation training (Benson, 1975; Benson et al., 1974). Benson's (1975, p. 468) list includes (a) mental device ("a constant stimulus"), (b) passive attitude ("one should not worry how well he [or she] is performing"), (c) decreased muscle tonus ("a comfortable posture"), and (d) quiet environment ("decreased environmental stimuli").

Mental device. In behavioral terms, this concerns observational behavior that, in one form or another, is included in all procedures. Trainees are routinely instructed to attend to some low-intensity regularly occurring event (a constant stimulus) such as their own breathing, proprioceptive sensations in their muscles, a biofeedback signal, or the trainer's voice.

Passive attitude. This translates into verbal instructions to ignore distractions, to continue observing the constant stimulus, and to avoid evaluating one's performance. Even procedures that provide feedback on performance emphasize that this information is constructive rather than evaluative in the sense of judging success or failure. Trainees may be instructed to repeat these rules to themselves.

Decreased muscle tonus. This refers to motoric behavior, which may be measured in terms of EMG, observation of the trainee's postures, or asking for a self-report. Relaxed muscles is implied, if not directly trained, by all methods.

Quiet environment. This characterizes the training setting regardless of method and, again, refers to observational behavior. This factor enhances the trainee's observation of the constant stimulus and minimizes observation of distracting stimuli.

Rules for Relaxation

An additional feature common to all relaxation training methods, not explicitly mentioned by Benson, is the rationale provided to the trainee. The rationale may be termed the "rules" for relaxation because it provides a verbal statement of the contingencies for engaging in the behaviors requested by the trainer. Rules are a statement of the contingent relationships between the antecedents, behaviors, and consequences (Poppen, 1989).

In essence, the trainee is instructed that if in various situations (antecedents) he or she engages in relaxation (behavior), then beneficial outcomes (consequences) will occur. The consequences of relaxation often are delayed or accrue only after a lengthy period of practice, and an important function of the rule is to bridge the gap between behavioral practice and the delayed benefits. The trainer also may include a description of the mechanism by which relaxation produces the desired outcome such as a description of physiological or cognitive structures.

Another rule, usually implicit, can be summed up by the statement, "My approval is contingent on your following my instructions." The trainer is seen as an expert, with special knowledge and skills, and is a potent reinforcing agent. His or her approval is an immediate consequence that keeps the trainee on task and also helps bridge the gap between relaxed behavior and its delayed benefits.

These rules become part of the trainee's verbal repertoire, allowing direction of his or her own behavior in the absence of the trainer. A trainee's understanding of a procedure is inferred from the degree to which he or she can repeat and follow these rules. This self-direction seldom is explicitly monitored.

Self-report is another feature common to all training methods. The exact format varies from rating on a numerical scale to narrative descriptions of subjective feelings. Trainers should recognize that self-report is influenced not only by covert feelings of relaxation but also by the social contingencies of the training situation. There may be some degree of compliance to the implied instruction, "Tell me you are relaxed."

The effect of these general forms of instructional control, sometimes termed "placebo" or "suggestion," raises concern as to whether relaxation procedures have any specific effects (Benson & Friedman, 1985; Holmes, 1984; Peveler & Johnston, 1986). Studies employing placebo procedures have found effects comparable with those of more active treatments. For example, Sapp (1996) found nondirective supportive counseling to be statistically more effective than progressive relaxation or "cognitive-behavioral hypnosis" in reducing test anxiety for undergraduate students, although progressive relaxation was more effective for graduate students. Borkovec and Costello (1993) also found therapeutic effects of nondirective counseling on generalized anxiety disorder, but cognitive therapy and progressive relaxation procedures produced larger and more long-lasting outcomes. Nonspecific factors such as expectancy of benefit, belief in treatment effectiveness, or faith in the therapist can be regarded as verbal rules that are a common feature of all relaxation procedures.

Distinctive Features of Relaxation Training Methods

In light of the four-modality taxonomy of behavior presented here, it is apparent that the various relaxation training methods differ in their emphases on particular response modalities. A similar point was made by Lehrer et al. (1994). Their account differs in that their focus is on the expected outcome of training rather than on the actual behavior of the trainee. For example, they term autogenic training an "autonomic" procedure because the target is warming the hands, whereas the system here classifies it as a "verbal" procedure because the trainee engages in verbal behavior.

Table 1.2 outlines the focus of several of the more common relaxation training procedures. Although each method targets a specific response in one or two of the behavioral modalities, there usually is an implicit assumption that training affects other responses both within the targeted modality and across modalities. It is implicit that each method treats relaxation as a response class, as described in the previous section, in which strengthening one member also strengthens the others.

Progressive Relaxation Training

This method emphasizes motoric behavior and covert observation of proprioceptive stimuli. Jacobson's (1929/1938) original procedure consisted of instructions to systematically tense and release dozens of muscle groups throughout the body and to observe the associated covert sensations. Trainees received several hour-long training sessions each week for several months and instructions to practice on their own for a couple hours each day. Wolpe (1958) developed an

Table 1.2:　　Behavioral Targets of Several Relaxation
　　　　　　　　　Training Methods

Training Method	Behavior Modality			
	Motoric	Verbal	Visceral	Observational
Progressive relaxation	Tense-release exercise, muscle tension[a]	Rules, self-report	—	Breathing, proprioceptive stimuli[a]
Behavioral relaxation	Postures, muscle tension[a]	Rules, self-report, labels[a]	Breathing	Postures, breathing, proprioceptive stimuli[a]
Electro-myography biofeedback	Muscle tension[a]	Rules, self-report	—	Feedback signal, Proprioceptive stimuli[a]
Thermal biofeedback	—	Rules, self-report	Vasodilation[a]	Feedback signal, warm feeling[a]
Meditation	Comfortable posture	Rules, self-report, mantra[a]	Breathing	Breathing, mantra[a]
Autogenic training	—	Rules, self-report, phrases[a]	Breathing, vasodilation[a]	Visceral stimuli,[a] proprioceptive stimuli[a]
Hypnosis	—	Rules, self-report	—	Sensory and proprioceptive stimuli[a]
Guided imagery	—	Rules, self-report	—	Sensory, visceral, and proprioceptive stimuli[a]

a. Covert behavior.

abbreviated form of Jacobson's lengthy procedure. Bernstein and Borkovec's (1973) manual has provided standardized instructions and exercises, facilitating research on this procedure. The goal of all forms is to teach observational skills, allowing trainees to be aware of even slight feelings of tension and to teach motoric skills, allowing the rapid reduction of that tension. Trainees are not encouraged to verbally echo the instructions, and the common use of audiotapes for practice maintains external verbal control.

Behavioral Relaxation Training

This procedure, which is described completely in Chapter 3, also emphasizes motoric behavior. In this case, the motoric behavior is overt, allowing observation by both the trainer and trainee. This avoids the "problem of privacy" (Skinner, 1969), in which the trainer attempts to teach discriminations of events to which he or she has no direct access. The trainee is instructed to observe his or her overt postures as well as the covert proprioceptive sensations and other feelings of relaxation that accompany them. Verbal definitions and "labels" of relaxed postures are provided, and these may be covertly echoed by the trainee and employed during practice on his or her own. Visceral behavior is included as slowed breathing, and diaphragmatic breathing instruction also may be employed.

EMG Biofeedback

This procedure also targets motoric behavior (Budzynski & Stoyva, 1969). The trainee alters covert muscle activity and observes the changes in a public stimulus that parallels the private event. An attempt to wean the trainee from control by the external signal sometimes is made by incorporating feedback-free trials and instructing the trainee to continue whatever he or she was doing during the feedback (Olton & Noonberg, 1980). In some instances, the trainee may be asked to observe the covert sensations of reduced tension, but this often is implied rather than directly instructed. Generalization within the motoric response class, from the trained muscle site to other muscle groups, has been reported in some experimental investigations but has not been found in others (Qualls & Sheehan, 1981; Tarler-Benlolo, 1978). The variables responsible for general or specific effects of EMG biofeedback training are unknown, although the use of verbal instructions has been suggested as a major factor (Qualls & Sheehan, 1981). Another variable may be that the trainee can shift his or her posture to achieve lowered EMG levels in the training site, which may inadvertently change EMG activity in other parts of the body as well (Poppen, Hanson, & Ip, 1988; Schilling & Poppen, 1983).

Thermal Biofeedback

This procedure focuses on visceral behavior, namely the dilation of peripheral vasculature (Sargent, Green, & Walters, 1973). The trainee is provided with a public signal that reflects minute changes in peripheral temperature. He or she is instructed to find some way in which to control the signal and to thereby control his or her vascular responses. Although the achievement of peripheral temperature control is well documented, disagreement remains as to whether the trainee engages in the behavior directly or first engages in behavior in another modality that mediates the vascular change (Bacon & Poppen, 1985; King & Montgomery, 1980; Miller, 1978; Olton & Noonberg, 1980; Taub & Emurian, 1976). All four response modalities have been suggested as candidates for mediating temperature control—motoric behavior in the form of muscular relaxation (King & Montgomery, 1980), verbal behavior in the form of autogenic phrases (Blanchard & Andrasik, 1985), visceral behavior in the form of breathing control (Bacon & Poppen, 1985), and observational behavior in the form of visual imagery (Blanchard & Andrasik, 1985). Biofeedback training for other visceral responses—such as heart rate, blood pressure, and skin conductance—is subject to the same considerations of mediation (Miller, 1978; Silver & Blanchard, 1978).

Meditation

This method targets verbal, visceral (breathing), and observational behavior (Benson, 1975). The trainer provides a sonorous syllable, the "mantra," which may be alleged to have special properties or be as mundane as the word "one." The trainee is instructed to covertly repeat the syllable with each exhalation and to observe his or her verbal and breathing behavior. The trainee is instructed to passively observe his or her behavior rather than to actively strive to achieve some result. Because the focus is on covert behavior, the trainer must rely on public accompaniments (e.g., closed eyes, slow and regular breathing), self-report, and physiological measures to assess progress. There exists an extensive literature supporting the effects of meditation training on decreasing muscle tension and autonomic arousal. However, a critical review of the research has asserted that such changes are no greater than those achieved by asking participants to rest quietly (Holmes, 1984). Thus, meditation may simply be a means of providing people with the social contingencies to systematically take a rest break. Indeed, proper controls for such effects are needed in all relaxation outcome research.

Autogenic Training

This procedure targets verbal and observational behavior (Schultz & Luthe, 1969). The trainer provides a series of statements concerning heaviness, warmth, and calmness in various parts of the body. The trainee covertly repeats the phrase and observes the described sensation. The statements refer to motoric and visceral activity (e.g., "My right hand is heavy," "My heartbeat is calm and regular"). It is assumed that such verbal and observational behavior directly influences responding in the visceral modality, but there is little controlled research supporting such direct self-instructional control. To take another example, repeating "My penis is erect" is no cure for impotence. Like meditation, autogenic training may only provide a rationale for systematic rest.

Hypnosis

This procedure has been used to influence a wide variety of behaviors including relaxation (Barber & Hahn, 1963; Paul, 1969; Sapp, 1996). The trainer provides verbal descriptions of motoric and observational behavior (e.g., "Imagine you are holding something heavy in your hand; now the hand and arm feel heavy as if the weight were pressing down") (Weitzenhoffer & Hilgard, 1962). Unlike autogenic training, the trainee is not instructed to covertly repeat the verbal behavior but rather to covertly engage in the motoric and observational behavior described. The observational behavior may include proprioceptive and visual imagery. The degree to which the trainee can be so engaged determines the success of the procedure. For example, when told that "Your hands and arms are so heavy, like they are made of stone, that you cannot lift them," the trainee who does not lift his or her hands when asked to do so is judged to be successfully hypnotized.

Guided Imagery

This is another verbal and observational procedure whereby the trainer describes scenes and actions in which the trainee imagines himself or herself engaging (Sheikh, 1983). It differs from autogenic training and hypnosis in that the trainee is instructed to construct a scene other than the training environment, such as a warm, tropical beach. The trainee is instructed to observe the "stimulus propositions" (Lang, 1977) of the scene in the sensory modalities of sight, sound, temperature, touch, and smell. It is similar to autogenic training and hypnosis in that the trainee is instructed to attend to the "response propositions" (Lang, 1977), that is, his or her own motoric and visceral behavior such as feeling relaxed and heavy with slow and regular pulse and breathing. Studies have shown that guided imagery instruction produces visceral and verbal responses appropriate to the scenes described (Carroll, Marzillier, & Merian, 1982; Dadds, Bovbjerg, Redd, & Cutmore, 1997; Lang, 1979).

Summary

Relaxation training methods include both common and specific features. Common components include a comfortable, distraction-free setting, general instructions to observe repetitive, low-intensity events, a rationale for engaging in training, the trainer-trainee social interaction, a belief in the efficacy of the procedure, and regular practice. Specific features are the motoric, verbal, visceral, or observational behaviors that each method targets for training. Changes in the target behaviors may be directly measured, indirectly inferred, or ignored by the trainer. (Issues in the measurement of relaxation are presented in Chapter 2.) Changes in categories of behavior not directly targeted often are assumed and sometimes assessed. Continuing research questions concern the effects of training in a particular behavior modality on other behavior within and across modalities, whether a general response class of relaxation across these modalities results from any or all of these training methods, and what effects relaxed behaviors may have on stress, pain, and anxiety problems. More specifically, do individuals experiencing problems in a particular behavior modality benefit most from learning relaxation that targets that modality? The review of Lehrer et al. (1994) tentatively suggested an affirmative answer.

2

Assessment of Relaxation

Clinicians and researchers who employ relaxation procedures rarely determine whether or not their clients and participants actually learn the skills they so assiduously try to teach. This observation, stated in the first edition of this book a decade ago, is equally true today. The prevailing emphasis continues to be on treatment outcome. Assessment efforts are directed toward measuring symptom reduction and improvement in functioning. An increasing literature is directed toward comparing various interventions to determine the relative effectiveness or the relative contribution of components of treatment packages that include relaxation training. Within this context, there is some concern with measuring the degree to which clients practice relaxation or other skills. However, assessment of proficiency in attaining skills rarely is done. This chapter first discusses why the measurement of relaxation proficiency is an important factor in determining treatment effectiveness.

On the other hand, many professionals believe that they do indeed keep track of their trainees' progress during relaxation instruction. This chapter also discusses some commonly employed measures employed during relaxation training and their limitations.

The main focus of this chapter is to present a method for assessing relaxation that can easily be incorporated into both clinical practice and research protocols. The Behavioral Relaxation Scale (BRS) is described along with scoring procedures and methods for observer training. It is recognized that the BRS does not provide a complete assessment tool, and the chapter concludes with a discussion of some issues in the multimodal assessment of relaxation.

WHY MEASURE?

The paradigm for teaching a skill involves the following steps on the part of the teacher:

1. Instruction.
2. Review performance of the student.
3. Reinforce progress.
4. Remediate errors.
5. Move to next stage of training.

Steps 3, 4, and 5 all depend on Step 2, which is assessment. This much is a truism in any educational enterprise and hardly bears repeating. However, teachers of relaxation just as routinely neglect measurement of their pupils' performance.

One reason for this neglect is the belief that such assessment is relatively unimportant. In this view, relaxation is an intermediate step and the important relation is between treatment and outcome. The clinician provides a treatment (e.g., autogenic training), and the client experiences an outcome (e.g., a reduction in headaches). This is the critical relationship, the researcher will say, and the clinician need not be concerned about what may be happening in between. Similarly, the researcher may compare one treatment (e.g., electromyographic [EMG] biofeedback) to another (e.g., attention-placebo) with the outcome again being headache reduction. Or, the researcher may compare a combination treatment (e.g., cognitive therapy and relaxation training) to each of the components individually. By careful control of extraneous variables, it is possible to demonstrate that the outcome is statistically more probable with one intervention compared to another.

The researcher's concern with probabilities raises a critical point. Relationships between treatments and outcomes never are black or white. Not all persons given autogenic training improve; not all persons given attention-placebo fail to improve. Both clinicians and researchers are constantly seeking to improve their odds, and looking at the direct effects of training provides one means of doing so. To use a medical analogy, in cases where a patient fails to improve, is it because the patient failed to take the pills or because the medication did not reach required levels in the bloodstream? Only by assessing the intermediate stage, the level of medication in the patient's system, can answers be obtained and treatment odds improved. The crucial relationship is not between the prescription of medication and outcome but rather is between biochemical action and outcome. Similarly, providing relaxation training is not the same thing as the client actually learning a skill and employing it in daily living. Assessing the client's proficiency in relaxation makes it possible to determine a dose-response relationship, a very powerful way of assessing treatment effectiveness.

Some investigators have begun to be concerned with treatment integrity, that is, the degree to which intervention is delivered "as advertised" (Gutkin, Holborn, Walker, & Anderson, 1992; Yeaton & Sechrest, 1981). To use the medical analogy, are the "pills" delivered in the prescribed manner? It is important, especially in research settings, that interventions are carried out as specified. However, providing treatment is not the same as the client learning a skill. Determining the relationship between relaxation treatment and outcome requires not only that the therapist administer training in the prescribed manner but also that the client demonstrate that relaxation has been learned. In addition, assessment of relaxation allows the trainer to provide guidance, correction, and reinforcement, in short, to teach rather than to merely instruct.

Another problem with looking at outcome as the only dependent measure is that often it is based on client self-report of subjective symptoms. The difficulties with this measure are discussed in the next section. Suffice it to say here that many variables in addition to the intervention can influence self-report. To strengthen the claim of treatment effectiveness, it is important to measure what happened to the client during training while he or she is available for objective observation. The degree of relaxation achieved in training is presumed to be a precursor of relaxation in the natural environment, which is one of the variables affecting self-report of symptoms. Thus, the assessment of relaxation gives the clinician and researcher one more handle by which to grasp the relationship between treatment and outcome.

CURRENT MEASURES OF RELAXATION

The assertion that professionals do not measure client behavior during training is based on reviews of the relaxation literature, which found that usually there is no mention of the degree to which participants became proficient in the target behavior of relaxation (Hillenberg & Collins, 1982; Lehrer, Carr, Sargunaraj, & Woolfolk, 1994; Luiselli, 1980; Luiselli, Marholin, D. Steinman, & W. Steinman, 1979). Many professionals might disagree with this assessment and insist that they do, in fact, measure client progress and proficiency but in informal and indirect ways. This may well be the case, but the reliance on cursory and incomplete measures only serves to prevent the development of effective assessment tools. Some currently employed approximations to relaxation measurement are discussed in this section.

Self-Report

Self-Report of Relaxation

The widespread notion of relaxation as an internal state leads to a reliance on the client as the primary observer of that state. Consequently, the trainer may gauge the client's progress by his or her answer to the question, "How did that go?" or "How do you feel?" Comments by the client such as "I feel like I am melted in the chair" or "I just can't seem to let myself go" are taken as primary data on the subjective state of relaxation. A somewhat more formal report system may be arranged, as in systematic desensitization, where the client signals with a lifted finger that a state of relaxation has been achieved or disturbed (Wolpe, 1958).

A more systematic procedure is to present the client with a numbered rating scale and ask for a report. The widely employed Subjective Unit of Disturbance Scale (SUDS) asks for a rating of anxiety or arousal from 0 to 100 (Wolpe & Lazarus, 1966). Although couched in terms of arousal, low ratings on the SUDS may be regarded as measures of calmness or relaxation. Schilling and Poppen (1983) employed a 7-point scale, with associated descriptors of relaxation and arousal, that has been used in many clinical and research settings (Appendix A). Other investigators have employed a 10-point scale (Norton, Holm, & McSherry, 1997; Wittrock, Blanchard, & McCoy, 1988) and a visual analog scale (Norton et al., 1997). The latter provides the trainee with a horizontal line with one end labeled *very tense* and the other end labeled *very relaxed.* The person simply makes a mark on the line; this is later converted to a numerical score by measuring the distance with a ruler from one end of the line to the mark.

Recently, two inventories have been developed to assess relaxation in ways other than simply rating the extent of relaxed feelings. The Relaxation Inventory is a 45-item questionnaire on which respondents endorse items describing feelings (Crist & Rickard, 1993; Crist, Rickard, Prentice-Dunn, & Barker, 1989). Three subscales were derived through factor analysis: Physiological Tension, Cognitive Tension, and Physical Assessment. Appropriate changes in subscale and total scores were obtained following progressive relaxation training, "imaginal" relaxation (in which participants were instructed to imagine themselves engaging in the relaxation exercises), and tension induction. The Revised Relaxation Wordlist is an 82-item inventory on which respondents rate the extent to which each word describes their relaxation experiences (Smith, Amutio, Anderson, & Aria, 1996). Responses by 940 practitioners of 11 different procedures (including progressive relaxation, Lamaze, yoga, and massage) were factor analyzed, yielding 5 to 14 factors depending on decision criteria. This instrument does not measure degree of relaxation but rather reflects various categories of relaxed feelings. These scales offer another means of assessing the verbal components of relaxation, although their reliability and relationship to other measures have yet to be examined.

It is necessary to include self-reports of internal events when working with verbal clients, but the relaxation trainer would do well to recognize the limitations of such behavior. The first limitation is what B. F. Skinner called "the problem of privacy" (Skinner, 1969). Stated simply, this problem is that people have difficulty discriminating and labeling internal stimuli because they lack corrective feedback from their environment. Little Johnny learns not to call a kitty "doggie" or to call the mailman "Daddy" when his mother observes the error and provides corrective consequences. But such accurate correction is not forthcoming in learning about internal events. We eventually arrive at a crude consensus about private stimuli through a slow process of metaphor (e.g., "I feel like a truck ran over me") and public accompaniments (e.g., "You seem down in the mouth"). But we never achieve the accuracy in discriminating such events that we do when people around us have direct access to, and can provide feedback on, what we are speaking about.

As an aside, we may note that the technology of biofeedback makes the client more precisely aware of internal events by allowing another observer, the therapist, to observe and label those events. For example, the therapist instructs the client, "You are becoming more tense when the tone becomes higher in pitch, and you are relaxing when the tone becomes lower and turns off." The therapist expresses approval when the tone decreases and concern when it increases. Both the social feedback and electronic feedback are necessary for the person to learn to accurately discriminate his or her levels of tension.

Another limitation of self-report is that it is so responsive to social contingencies, often to a greater extent than to internal stimuli. It is well documented that people often report feeling more relaxed after receiving some treatment that they are told is effective, even though no change has taken place in motoric or visceral modalities (Mathews, 1971; Norton et al., 1997; Qualls & Sheehan, 1981; Reinking & Kohl, 1975; Schilling & Poppen, 1983; Taylor & Lee, 1991). Conversely, people may report no change in feelings, even though muscle tension has actually decreased, when the procedure is labeled "physiological assessment" rather than "relaxation training" (Poppen, Hanson, & Ip, 1988). Part of what is termed a "placebo effect" is this change in verbal behavior in response to therapist instructions and approval.

Self-Report of Symptoms

The primary dependent variable in all therapy and most research endeavors involving relaxation is the reduction of the trainee's complaint. As discussed in the previous section, this focus on outcome may preclude measurement of relaxation. In some instances such as hypertension, spasmodic torticollis, and Raynaud's disease, the disorder can be measured objectively. But in most instances such as headache and other types of pain, anxiety, and panic, the therapist must depend on the client's report. This report may be systematically solicited, as in a "headache diary" (Blanchard & Andrasik, 1985), or more informally gathered (e.g., "Well, how's it going this week?"). The limitations concerning self-report of arousal and relaxation, described earlier, apply just as well to self-report of symptoms. Of particular concern are the social contingencies that serve to maintain such reports. For example, Fordyce (1976) documented the influence of social contingencies on verbal reports of both pain and other pain behaviors.

Whether the symptom is self-reported or objectively measured, the assumption is that it provides a measure of relaxation; that is, improvement in the symptom is taken to indicate that the client is relaxing successfully. In negative instances, it is not clear whether the client is not engaging in relaxation or whether relaxation is not having the desired effect. The latter instance merely points up a problem that is overlooked when the client does improve, namely, that the link between relaxation and symptom is conjectural at best, and the status of the symptom does not automatically reflect the proficiency or frequency with which the client engages in relaxation. The relationship between relaxation and symptom change is a matter greatly in need of experimental investigation, and research that lumps the two together adds little to our knowledge of this relationship. Even the clinician, whose primary interest is in symptomatic improvement, could provide better service if he or she knew the client's proficiency in relaxation. Such knowledge would aid the therapist in deciding whether or not to persist in relaxation training when little symptom change seems evident and in determining which aspect of treatment to continue, or to try with other clients, when positive gains are seen.

Physiological Measures

As discussed in Chapter 1, the internal stimuli about which people are presumed to be reporting when they describe their arousal and symptoms result from the covert activity of various motoric and visceral systems. In other instances, such as hypertension, the relevant physiological systems may be difficult to observe and exert little stimulus control over the client's verbal behavior. In either case, it would seem that a direct way of measuring relaxation is to measure physiological activity.

Several questions immediately arise. Which physiological systems should be measured? Under what conditions should measurement occur? How should these conditions be induced and themselves measured? What is the relationship between the conditions under which physiological assessment can be carried out and the person's everyday living conditions? What is the reliability of such measures? How does one resolve conflicts between self-report and physiological measures?

Which Physiological Systems?

The answer to this question involves several considerations. Foremost among these is the particular disorder for which the client is seeking treatment. In many psychophysiological disorders, the target symptom suggests the system to be measured (Blanchard, 1981). Thus, for hypertension, one would measure blood pressure or perhaps a contributory system such as heart rate or transit time. For muscle-related pain such as tension headache, TMJ disorder, or lower back pain, EMG levels of regional musculature are appropriate. For panic attack and asthma, measures of respiration type, rate, and depth would be indicated.

Theoretical considerations also are important. For example, Benson (1975) conceptualized relaxation in terms of diminished energy expenditure and thus measured the body's exhaust gas, carbon dioxide. Other autonomic theories emphasize generalized sympathetic quiescence and measure electrodermal (EDR) activity (Javel & Denholtz, 1975). Theories that emphasize motoric behavior measure EMG levels in one or several muscle groups (Budzynski & Stoyva, 1969; Poppen & Maurer, 1982).

Another consideration is practical, in terms of the equipment and expertise at hand. Researchers, of course, should have adequate equipment to measure the variables of interest. Clinicians may be more restricted in what is available to them. Biofeedback-based treatment has the advantage of equipment that can provide assessment of the target physiological system if only trainers would bother to summarize the data from each session. When biofeedback is not employed, ethical treatment standards demand that practitioners invest in equipment and training sufficient to measure the physiological symptoms they are targeting.

Even when narrowed by these considerations, there are literally scores of physiological systems that present themselves for measurement. For example, a well-studied disorder such as tension headache may involve many head and neck muscles in addition to frontalis including temporalis, masseter, orbicularis occuli, sternocleidomastoid, and cervical trapezius. Perhaps measures of blood flow in these muscles, rather than electrical activity, would be more appropriate (Olton & Noonberg, 1980). Little is known about the interrelations and influences among the multiple physiological systems either within a modality (e.g., the muscular system) or across modalities (e.g., the respiratory and cardiovascular systems). For example, there is considerable evidence that biofeedback-trained reduction of frontalis EMG levels does not influence nearby musculature (Qualls & Sheehan, 1981). On the other hand, such training often is associated with changes in cardiovascular and respiratory activity (Qualls & Sheehan, 1981). It is safe to say that our knowledge of physiological systems in relaxation is miniscule. Rather than throwing up one's hands in despair at this chasm of ignorance, both the clinician and researcher are advised to roll up their sleeves and begin to build. By including systematic measures of physiological activity during relaxation training as well as during pre- and posttraining, in the home environment as well as in the clinic, and in unusual response modalities as well as in the traditional ones, the gaps in knowledge will be slowly knit together.

Under What Conditions?

Physiological measurement may be carried out in a variety of situations. If an objective of relaxation treatment is to change the activity level in a particular physiological system, then it is necessary to measure that system while the client is engaging in relaxation. Changes in the measure from pretreatment levels over the course of training provide important feedback to the clinician and perhaps also to the client. In the laboratory, such data provide evidence of the integrity of the independent variable and should be routinely gathered and reported.

A related objective of relaxation treatment is to reduce the arousal of a particular physiological system under stressful conditions or to speed recovery of the system after stress. To verify this objective, one can measure physiological activity during and after some demand placed on the client. The most commonly employed laboratory stressors are "psychological" demands (e.g., serial subtraction, emotional imagery) and "physical" demands (e.g., the cold pressor test, i.e., placing the client's hand or foot in ice water) (Blanchard, 1981). As Blanchard (1981) noted, "This seems a very promising avenue of research but has received only limited attention thus far" (p. 257). A good example of this approach was shown by Cole, Pomerleau, and Harris (1992), who found that progressive relaxation training was associated with decreased blood pressure in cardiac patients only when it was carried out during a specific stressful event. Another study found that the blood pressure response to a laboratory stressor was ameliorated by relaxation training, but this effect could be eliminated by administration of the endorphin-blocking agent naltrexone (McCubbin et al., 1996).

The similarity between physiological activity in a clinic or laboratory setting and the client's everyday living situation often is assumed but rarely is investigated. The underpinning of much relaxation therapy is that the physiological changes achieved in training will be manifest in the client's natural environment. The small amount of evidence for this assumption is supportive. Agras and his associates showed that blood pressure reductions achieved in the clinic with relaxation training persisted in the patients' work and home environments (Agras, Taylor, & Kraemer, 1980; Southam, Agras, Taylor, & Kraemer, 1982). However, home and work measures were carried out only after treatment had been completed and hence do not show concurrence between training and generalization effects. Poppen et al. (1988) demonstrated that EMG reductions, accomplished with biofeedback training while students engaged in reading, concurrently generalized to their usual places of study. Although these early results are promising, it is obvious that much more research needs to be done, encompassing the whole spectrum of disorders treated with the wide variety of relaxation training methods. Such research is an integral part of the task of verifying the utility of particular training methods for particular disorders.

How Reliable?

Some researchers have questioned the reliability of physiological measures. Arena and colleagues found frontalis EMG levels to be reliable across a variety of conditions (baseline, instructions to relax, and mental arithmetic) when assessments were performed up to 1 month apart (Arena, Blanchard, Andrasik, Cotch, & Myers, 1983). Hand temperature and heart rate were found to be similarly reliable, but only for assessments no more than 1 week apart. Measures of EDR activity, cephalic vasomotor response, and forearm flexor EMG levels were generally inconsistent. As the authors recognized, the implications of this research for clinical populations remain to be determined.

What Is the Relationship Between Measures?

The discrepancies between physiological measures and self-report have been noted in preceding sections. The fact that self-report often is the product of social contingencies rather than an accurate response to internal stimuli points up the importance of assessing multiple dimensions of relaxation. Where discrepancies arise, the trainer should be alert to what may be the important controlling stimuli for each class of behavior. Discrepancies may indicate, for example, that pain reports are controlled by social contingencies or that inappropriate physiological systems are being monitored. In either case, a change of treatment strategies may be indicated.

The relationship between various physiological measures also is subject to investigation. The early classic work of John and Beatrice Lacey suggested that automatic response classes were idiosyncratic when participants were exposed to stressful situations (Lacey & Lacey, 1958); that is, across individuals, correlations of various measures were zero, whereas within each individual, stable patterns often were apparent. It is not known whether this same idiosyncrasy holds for responses to relaxation training.

Measurement of Process

A common substitute for measuring relaxation itself is to count the number of training sessions. Particularly with the advent of standardized relaxation programs, researchers often simply state that the participant received a certain number of sessions of a particular procedure (Hillenberg & Collins, 1982). In many instances, the entire program is put on audiotape and the participant may not be observed directly. Standardized relaxation programs represent an advance in that they allow a specification of what was done to the client in a manner that can be communicated and replicated. However, "canned" procedures seduce the trainer into neglecting direct observation of effects on the client.

Hillenberg and Collins (1983) added auditory signals to a home practice relaxation tape and asked participants to report the number of tones they heard. Although this procedure provided a measure of compliance of at least listening to the tape, it did not assess either practice or proficiency. A refinement of this approach employed a pressure transducer and home computer program that recorded the amount of time the participants laid on a mat coupled with a hand switch that they were instructed to operate each time they engaged in a tense-release exercise recorded on audiotape (Gutkin et al., 1992). Criteria for "appropriate practice" were determined by comparing computer outputs to the duration and timing of the exercises on the audiotapes. With three headache patients, these researchers found that the amount of headache reduction was related to the degree of appropriate practice during the assessment period. However, there was no relationship at a 1-year follow-up, when the person who had practiced the least reported the greatest headache improvement. Although it is important to verify home practice, it also seems important to determine the patient's skill level.

A common research assumption is that when a standard, fixed number of training sessions is provided, everyone receives the same "dose" of relaxation. However, a fixed number of sessions is no substitute for measuring the client's response to the training program. Following the medication analogy, the same dose of a drug does not produce the same blood level in all patients. Individual client differences in response to relaxation training are a well-known fact of life to researchers and clinicians. Providing a measure of the duration of training suggests a homogeneity that can be misleading.

Some research questions may be answered by specifying a particular amount of training. For example, in comparing two or more treatment regimes in their effects on a particular disorder, it is standard operating procedure to control for amount of therapist contact by providing equal numbers of sessions and equal session length for all treatments. Individual differences are not of direct concern and are treated as random error variability in statistical analysis. An alternative design would be to train participants to a particular criterion of proficiency by different methods. The number of trials (training sessions) to the criterion would provide a measure of efficacy of the various methods. Individuals who learn quickly or slowly with the various procedures could be examined in more detail for idiosyncratic variables that are related to their success or failure. Such a design is closer to clinical practice and would provide data of interest and use to the clinician (Poppen, 1983).

Clinicians are less likely to be bound to a fixed number of relaxation training sessions and to rely more on proficiency criteria. Yet, the proficiency criteria are likely to be the subjective self-reports of arousal level and symptoms discussed earlier. Clinicians also make use of audiotapes for both office training and home practice. Often the only measure of the use of these tapes is self-report; the methods of Hillenberg and Collins (1983) or Gutkin et al. (1992) perhaps could be adapted for use in a clinical setting. But advances in the technology of training delivery methods do not relieve the trainer of the responsibility of determining whether that technology is working. To borrow an example from education, do we award a student a diploma for sitting through 12 years of schooling or for demonstrating proficiency in specific academic skills? Too often, we settle for the process criterion because we have no measure of proficiency.

Informal Observation

Many clinicians, as a result of years of working with clients, are able to tell how relaxed or tense a person is and to detect discrepancies between a client's self-report and these nonverbal cues. It is common for a client at the beginning of training to state that he or she is relaxed and comfortable, whereas the clinician can just "see" that the client is not. Similarly, a researcher may see that a participant is just not "getting it" despite the most assiduous administration of the relaxation protocol. To what is the experienced trainer responding? Such wisdom may be difficult to communicate and may be ascribed to "intuition" or "clinical acumen."

If one closely reads the descriptions provided by the pioneers in relaxation such as Wolpe (1958, 1973), Bernstein and Borkovec (1973), and particularly Jacobson (1929/1938), then one finds clues as to what features of the client the clinician is responding. This is getting close to the heart of behavioral relaxation assessment. Our basic premise is that the client emits certain behavior that tells the observer how relaxed or aroused he or she is. The following section describes the nature of these relaxed behaviors.

Summary

Several approximate measurements of the complex behavior called relaxation exist in the clinic and laboratory. These include self-report, physiological assessment, process measurements, and informal observation. But systematic efforts to monitor the progress of trainees are rare. This state of affairs may exist because trainers accept the current measurement procedures as sufficient or because no good alternative is available. The preceding sections have described the shortcomings of current measurement procedures. The following section presents a different procedure for assessing relaxation that, although not solving all the problems, offers the clinician and researcher an easy method for measuring the motoric domain of relaxation.

THE BEHAVIORAL RELAXATION SCALE

Measurement of relaxation, as discussed in the preceding sections, usually is based on the premise that relaxation is an internal state. Primarily, self-report has been used to measure a covert, undifferentiated "state" of relaxation, and physiological recording has been used to measure covert motoric and visceral aspects of this state. The basic premise of the BRS is that a relaxed person engages in overt motoric behavior that is characteristic of relaxation. It is possible for an external observer to take note of these behaviors and to judge how relaxed the client is. At this point, the concern is only with relaxation in the training situation. In later sections, the issue of relaxation assessment in other types of situations is addressed. Also, the BRS is primarily a measure of the motoric behavior aspects of relaxation. Description of a more complete multimodal assessment procedure concludes this chapter.

A Brief History of the BRS

As one reads the classic work of Edmund Jacobson, one is struck by the descriptive detail of what to look for in his or her patients. His text is accompanied by many photographs showing the trainer what the outcome of his or her efforts should look like. Similarly, other investigators have presented phenomenological descriptions of what transpires as a person becomes relaxed along with hints on how to assess it. Wolpe (1958, 1973) and Bernstein and Borkovec (1973) have been particularly helpful in this respect. The contributions of Arnold Lazarus, who instructed the author in the arcane art of relaxation, also should be acknowledged. Many years of teaching relaxation, as well as teaching students to teach relaxation, resulted in some "rules of thumb" for assessing relaxation.

Don Schilling was the first to apply these rules of thumb in a systematic fashion when he undertook relaxation training with "predelinquent" boys. Progressive relaxation training had resulted in boys who were good at the "tensing" part but poor at "releasing." Showing some creative behaviorism, Schilling decided to teach the boys to "look relaxed." Sure enough, the children not only could look relaxed, they reported that they felt relaxed and exhibited a calm demeanor after each training session. All that remained was to work out a specific list of behaviors and to formally test the reliability of observation and the relation to other measures. That list became the BRS.

Ten Relaxed Behaviors

The BRS consists of a description of 10 postures and activities characteristic of a fully relaxed person whose body is fully supported by a reclining chair or similar device. First, these behaviors are described in words and pictures. Next, a method for systematically observing them is presented.

Each behavior consists of an overt posture or activity of a particular region of the body. To enhance discrimination, both relaxed behaviors and some commonly occurring unrelaxed behaviors are presented for each item.

1. Head

Relaxed. The head is motionless and supported by the recliner with the nose in the midline of the body. Body midline usually can be determined by clothing features such as shirt buttons or apex of V neckline. Part of the nostrils and the underside of the chin are visible (see Figure 2.1A).

Unrelaxed. The following is (are) observed: (a) movement of the head, (b) head turned from body midline with the entire nose beyond midline (Figure 2.1B), (c) head tilted downward with the nostrils and underside of the chin not visible (Figure 2.1B), (d) head unsupported by the recliner (Figure 2.1C), and/or (e) head tilted upward with the entire underside of the chin visible (Figure 2.1D).

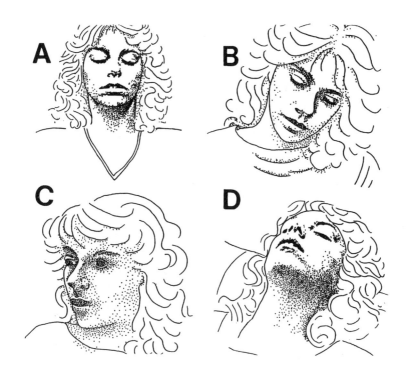

Figure 2.1: Postures of the Head: (A) Relaxed, (B-D) Unrelaxed

2. Eyes

Relaxed. The eyelids are lightly closed with a smooth appearance and no motion of the eyes beneath the eyelids (see Figure 2.2A).

Unrelaxed. The following is (are) observed: (a) eyes open, (b) eyelids closed but wrinkled or fluttering (Figure 2.2B), and/or (c) eyes moving under the eyelids.

3. Mouth

Relaxed. The lips are parted at the center of the mouth from ¼ inch to 1 inch (7-25 mm) with the front teeth also parted (see Figure 2.3A).

Unrelaxed. The following is (are) observed: (a) teeth in occlusion, (b) lips closed (Figure 2.3B), (c) mouth open greater than 1 inch (25 mm) (in most cases, the corners of the mouth will separate when the

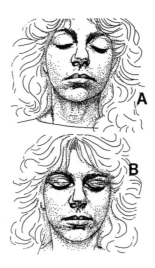

Figure 2.2: Postures of the Eyes: (A) Relaxed, (B) Unrelaxed

mouth is open beyond the criterion (Figure 2.3C), and/or (d) tongue motion (e.g., licking lips).

4. Throat

Relaxed. There is an absence of motion (see Figure 2.4).

Unrelaxed. There is any type of movement in the throat and neck (e.g., swallowing or other larynx action, twitches in the neck muscles).

5. Shoulders

Relaxed. Both shoulders appear rounded and transect the same horizontal plane. They rest against the recliner with no motion other than respiration (see Figure 2.5A).

Unrelaxed. The following is (are) observed: (a) movement of shoulders, (b) shoulders on a diagonal plane (Figure 2.5B), and/or (c) shoulders are raised or lowered so as not to appear rounded (Figure 2.5C).

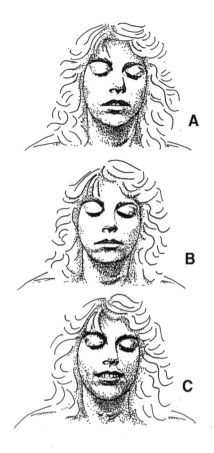

Figure 2.3: Postures of the Mouth: (A) Relaxed, (B-C) Unrelaxed

6. Body

Relaxed. The torso, hips, and legs are symmetrical around midline, resting against the chair, with no movement (see Figure 2.6A).

Unrelaxed. The following is (are) observed: (a) any movement of the torso other than respiration, (b) twisting of torso, hips, or legs out of midline (Figure 2.6B), (c) any movement of the hips, legs, or arms that does not result in movement of feet or hands (these are scored separately), and/or (d) any part of the back, buttocks, or legs not supported by the recliner.

Figure 2.4: Relaxed Posture of the Throat

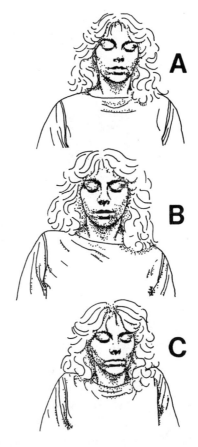

Figure 2.5: Postures of the Shoulders: (A) Relaxed, (B-C) Unrelaxed

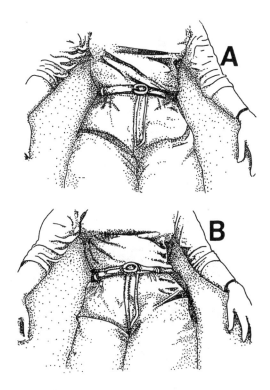

Figure 2.6: Postures of the Body: (A) Relaxed, (B) Unrelaxed

7. Hands

Relaxed. Both hands are resting on the armrest of the chair or on the lap with palms down and the fingers curled in a claw-like fashion. The fingers are sufficiently curled if a pencil can pass freely beneath the highest point of the arc other than the thumb (see Figure 2.7A).

Unrelaxed. The following is (are) observed: (a) hands gripping the armrest, (b) fingers extended and straight (Figure 2.7B), (c) fingers curled so that nails touch the surface of the armrest (Figure 2.7C), (d) fingers intertwined, and/or (e) movement of the hands.

8. Feet

Relaxed. The feet are pointed away from each other at an angle between 60° and 90° (see Figure 2.8A).

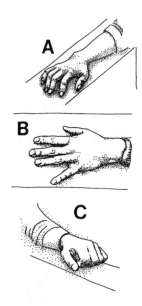

Figure 2.7: Postures of the Hands: (A) Relaxed, (B-C) Unrelaxed

Unrelaxed. The following is (are) observed: (a) movement of feet, (b) feet pointing vertically or at an angle less than 60° (Figure 2.8B), (c) feet pointing out at an angle greater than 90° (Figure 2.8C), (d) feet crossed at the ankles (Figure 2.8D), and/or (e) one heel placed more than 1 inch (25 mm) ahead of or behind the other.

9. Quiet

Relaxed. There are no vocalizations or loud respiratory sounds.

Unrelaxed. There is any type of verbalization or vocalization (e.g., talking, sighing, grunting, snoring, gasping, coughing).

10. Breathing

Relaxed. The breath frequency is less than that observed during baseline with no breathing interruptions. One breath equals one complete inhale-exhale cycle. A breath is counted if any part of the inhale occurs on the cue starting the observation interval and any part of the exhale occurs on the cue ending the observation interval (see how to score breathing in section titled "Scoring the BRS").

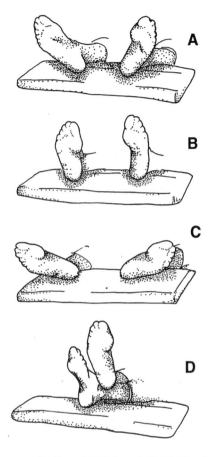

Figure 2.8: Postures of the Feet: (A) Relaxed, (B-D) Unrelaxed

Unrelaxed. The following is (are) observed: (a) breath frequency is equal to or greater than that during baseline and/or (b) any irregularity that interrupts the regular rhythm of breathing (e.g., coughing, laughing, yawning, sneezing).

All relaxed behaviors are shown together in Figure 2.9. The trainee can be scanned from head to feet on a systematic basis to measure relaxation, as presented in the next section.

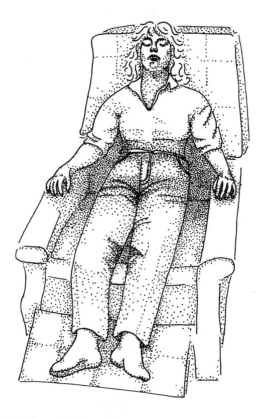

Figure 2.9: Full View of Relaxed Postures

Using the BRS

One of the main uses of the BRS is to assess the degree of relaxation attained by a client participating in a particular relaxation training procedure. As Chapter 3 describes, the BRS is an integral part of a relaxation training method called Behavioral Relaxation Training (BRT). However, the BRS is useful by itself as a dependent measure for any relaxation training procedure chosen by the trainer. In its standard form, the BRS requires that the training be carried out with the trainee seated in a reclining chair or similar device. Modifications for use with the client seated in a straight-back chair are presented later.

Duration of the Observation Period

The BRS requires an observation period, usually at the conclusion of a relaxation training session. It also may be employed at the beginning of a session as a pretreatment measure. The duration of the observation period must be several minutes. We have employed durations of 3, 5, and 10 minutes. The longer the period, the more representative sample of relaxed behavior will be obtained. But considerations of time constraints and trainee characteristics are important and should be evaluated for each application. Five minutes is sufficient for most purposes.

Each minute of the observation period is divided into three intervals: a 30-second interval to observe breathing rate, a 15-second interval to observe the other nine items on the BRS, and a 15-second interval to record the observations on the BRS Score Sheet. The BRS Score Sheet is included as Appendix B. Copies of the BRS Score Sheet should be made for the trainer to use in assessing relaxation.

Reactivity

Any behavioral observation procedure may be reactive if the person is aware of the observation; that is, the act of measurement may influence the behavior being measured, resulting in inaccurate assessment. We have found two major areas of reactivity in employing the BRS that the user should be aware of and take steps to reduce. The two reactive features of the BRS are the discriminability of the observation period and concern over "being watched."

The discriminability of the observation period is an important factor in gathering accurate measures. It usually is desirable to measure relaxation in the absence of other interactions with the client. Observation typically is carried out in silence, which may provide a cue to the client about a change in conditions; that is, if relaxation training has employed some sort of signal or instruction administered to the client (e.g., biofeedback, progressive muscle relaxation) and this presentation suddenly ends, then the client may be alerted that the session is about to end. This could disrupt relaxation. We typically instruct clients that at the conclusion of training, they will be asked to relax "on their own" for several minutes while we assess the effectiveness of training. They are instructed to continue whatever they have been doing in training until we tell them the session is over. This is sufficient for most people. However, we have found in working with "hyperactive" children (Chapter 4) that it is necessary to allow a couple of minutes at the conclusion of training for the children to "settle down" before collecting relaxation measures. It also is possible to incorporate an observation period within the training session or to continue to administer treatment until the end of the session so that there are no changes to alert the client.

Concern about being watched is another reactive aspect of the BRS. This problem, although not widespread, is most evident in the initial stages of training when baseline measures are being collected. It is at this time when the procedures are the most unfamiliar to the trainee and also the time when the trainee is most likely to have his or her eyes open, watching the trainer watch him or her. This can be particularly unnerving. "Eyes closed" is one of the items on the BRS, and instructions to the participant to close his or her eyes would be a confound in the baseline period of a research project. In clinical practice, where baseline data collection usually is not so rigorous, it does no harm to ask the client to close his or her eyes. This merely inflates the baseline relaxation score by 10% and can be noted accordingly.

In addition, the trainee should be instructed in the rationale given at the start of their training procedure that it is necessary to measure the effects of the training and that, therefore, he or she will be observed. The emphasis should be that it is the training procedure that is being measured, rather than how well the trainee is performing, to avoid undue performance pressure. Examples of such instructions are given in a later section. Generally, the trainee becomes more at ease as training progresses and observation is accepted as part of the procedure.

Where facilities permit, it may be possible to observe the trainee through a one-way window or to use a video camera to view or record an observation period. Not seeing the observer may put the trainee more at ease. When this is done, ethical practice requires that the person be informed that observation is taking place. In all cases, either clinical or research, every effort should be made to establish good rapport between the trainer and trainee and to assure the latter that confidentiality always is maintained.

Setting

The observer should place himself or herself in a position to obtain a full and unobstructed view of the trainee. Because symmetry around midline is an important aspect of several items on the BRS, the observer should not be seated completely to one side of the trainee. To best observe symmetry, the observer may sit at the foot of the chair, directly facing the trainee. However, if the client's feet are elevated, then the feet may block the observer's view of breathing, body, or hands. Also, if the trainee is wearing a skirt, then such a position may seem improper. We have found that placing the observer to one side of the foot of the recliner, at the "5 o'clock" or "7 o'clock" position, provides a good view of symmetry and all behaviors listed on the BRS. The observer should be seated about 1 meter from the trainee. The room should be lighted well enough to permit observation of small movements, but the light should not be so bright as to disrupt relaxation. All these considerations are especially important in the placement of a video camera or a one-way window, both of which tend to restrict observation.

Scoring the BRS

The observer requires a timing device to divide each minute of the observation period into appropriate scoring intervals. One option is to use an electronic stopwatch attached to a clipboard holding the BRS Score Sheet. When using a stopwatch, the observer must be careful not to avert his or her eyes from the client and perhaps miss the occurrence of unrelaxed behavior. Alternatively, a large battery-operated clock with a sweep second hand or digital readout of seconds may be placed just behind the client, allowing the observer to view the clock as he or she scans the client. Another method is to put time cues on an audiocassette tape, which then can be played by the observer and heard unobtrusively through a small earphone.

Before starting the observation period, the observer should write in the client's name or identification code on the BRS Score Sheet (Appendix B). The date, time, session number, and other relevant training data also should be written down. The client's baseline breathing rate, determined from pretraining baseline sessions, should be written in the box at the top of the BRS Score Sheet. The method used to determine a person's baseline breathing rate is described in a later section.

BRS scoring involves an interval recording method of behavioral observation. The presence or absence of a particular event during a specified interval of time is recorded; occurrences outside that specified interval are ignored.

The first behavior scored in each interval is breathing. With the onset of each minute of the observation period, the observer determines whether or not the client is inhaling. If so, then the observer counts this as the start of an inhale-exhale cycle; if not, then the observer waits until the next inhale before beginning the count. Each inhale-exhale cycle is counted as one breath. When the timing device indicates that 30 seconds have elapsed, the observer stops counting breaths. If the client is exhaling at the end of the breathing observation interval, then the cycle is counted as a complete breath. If the client is inhaling at the end of the interval, then that breath is not counted. The observer writes the number of breaths in the box at the top of each column of the BRS Score Sheet in the row marked "breathing." If an interruption to breathing occurs (see description of unrelaxed breathing in section titled "Ten Relaxed Behaviors"), then the observer marks an "X" in the box.

For the 15 seconds following observation of breathing, the observer scans the client for any unrelaxed behavior in the other nine items listed on the BRS. If an unrelaxed behavior is observed, then the observer may silently repeat the one-word label for that behavior to himself or herself to aid recall until the end of the interval. If recall is a problem, then the observer may immediately circle the minus sign in the appropriate column of the BRS Score Sheet in the row of the particular item noted. This should be done quickly so as not to miss other occurrences of unrelaxed behavior.

For the final 15 seconds of each minute, the observer circles the minus signs in the appropriate rows for any unrelaxed behaviors observed in the preceding 15-second interval. If no unrelaxed behaviors were noted, then the appropriate plus signs are circled. The breathing rate written in the small box at the top of each column is compared to the baseline breathing rate. If the rate is less than baseline, then the plus sign is circled; if the rate is equal to or greater than baseline or if an interruption occurred, then the minus sign is circled.

This process is repeated for each successive minute of the observation period, designated by columns on the BRS Score Sheet.

The BRS score for each observation period is a percentage based on the number of behaviors scored as relaxed or unrelaxed divided by the total number of observations. The number of relaxed behaviors is the total number of plus signs that were circled; the number of unrelaxed behaviors is the number of minus signs circled. If a 5-minute observation period is employed, then the total number of observations is 50 (5 minutes × 10 behaviors); if a 10-minute period is employed, then the total number of observations is 100. The BRS may be scored in either a negative (percentage unrelaxed) or positive (percentage relaxed) direction. "Percentage unrelaxed" is the total number of minus signs divided by the total number of observations; "percentage relaxed" is the total number of plus signs divided by the total number of observations. Negative scoring may be used to show a decline in unrelaxed behavior parallel to decreases in muscle tension (Schilling & Poppen, 1983). Positive scoring shows progress in a fashion more easily understood by the client. The trainer should choose a scoring method that best serves the requirements of the particular training situation.

Baseline Breathing Rate

A baseline rate must be established as the standard against which further breathing rates are measured. It is important to observe a sufficient number of intervals to obtain a representative sample of breathing rates. For research studies, we recommend a minimum of three 5-minute observation periods, a total of 15 measurement intervals. In clinical settings, it may be useful to employ a single baseline session of at least 15 minutes in which the client is told to relax as he or she normally does.

During baseline observation sessions, breathing is scored as described previously. The mean rate is then calculated by summing all the individual rates for each interval and dividing by the total number of observations. Intervals that were scored as "interruptions" are not included in calculating the mean breathing rate. Any fractional value for the mean breathing rate is "rounded up" to the next whole number. This value is then entered in the box at the top of the BRS Score Sheet as the "baseline breathing rate."

The astute reader will have observed that the BRS score for baseline sessions cannot be calculated until after a baseline breathing rate has been determined. Once the baseline breathing rate has been established, the BRS score for baseline sessions can then be calculated in the same way as it is for other sessions.

Training BRS Observers

The trainer wishing to use the BRS must be able to do so easily and accurately. Ease of use allows the BRS to be unobtrusively incorporated into the relaxation training routine. Accuracy is essential to make sure that the BRS does the job it is intended to do. In addition, when the BRS is employed in research settings, it is important to demonstrate that it is scored reliably, that is, that two or more observers observe and report the same events. In this regard, Boice (1983) reported that investigators employing behavioral observation routinely fail to evaluate the competence of their observers. Simply requiring observers to produce similar reports does not ensure accuracy or reliability. Training observers is itself an issue in behavioral technology (Johnston & Pennypacker, 1980).

On its face, the BRS appears straightforward and simple to learn and use. But this simplicity should not mislead the user into assuming that no background or training is necessary. It does, however, make such training relatively easy to accomplish. We have found the following training protocol, based on behavioral technology principles (Foster & Cone, 1986; Johnston & Pennypacker, 1980), to be effective in training clinical and research observers to accurately and reliably use the BRS.

Memorize the BRS Items

First, the observers must master the definitions of each of the 10 relaxed behaviors and the commonly seen unrelated behaviors, presented earlier in this chapter. In addition, the use of the BRS Score Sheet must be learned.

BRS Written Criterion Test

After memorizing the items, observers should pass a written test covering all BRS items. Observers are required to define the items and provide examples of relaxed and unrelaxed behaviors for each. Sample tests are provided in Appendix C. A 100% criterion of proficiency is recommended before proceeding with training.

Analog Relaxation Observation

Observers are now ready to score the items of the BRS with a live or videotaped model. If facilities permit, and if many observers need to be trained, then it is useful to construct a videotape that provides a standardized sequence of behaviors to be scored.

Individual items. For successive 30-second intervals, the observer monitors a single item of the BRS and scores it as relaxed or unrelaxed. A predetermined sequence of items is followed. The model (live or videotaped) emits relaxed behavior during a random 50% of the intervals and various unrelaxed behaviors during the other 50%. In addition to learning discrimination of the behaviors, this procedure trains the observer to keep track of time while observing the model. Practice should continue until 100% proficiency is achieved.

Multiple items. A 5-minute observation period is employed in which the observer scores successive 1-minute intervals for all 10 items on the BRS using the BRS Score Sheet. The model displays a predetermined sequence of relaxed and unrelaxed behaviors. Videotapes are particularly useful at this stage in that a series of 5-minute scenes can be employed and the observer's scores compared to the predetermined standard. If the scenes are done live, then the model must be skillful in following the predetermined sequence so that questions do not arise as to whether the model or observer was responsible for a disagreement. If live observation is employed, then it is best to have a trained primary observer simultaneously score the intervals and serve as a standard of comparison. Each of the 50 cells in the BRS Score Sheet for a 5-minute observation period are compared to the standard, and disagreements are explained. A videotape is useful in this regard because an interval in question can be replayed and differences in opinion resolved.

Live Relaxation Observation

If videotape has been employed in the previous step, then observation of a live model is now necessary. Comparisons of the observer's BRS scoring to a trained primary observer's scoring are carried out, and a reliability score is calculated. Reliability is expressed as a percentage in which the number of agreements between the two observers is divided by 50 (for a 5-minute period). Training should continue until reliability is consistently 90% or better. Disagreements should be discussed and clarified.

Client Observation

The observer can now score an actual client in conjunction with another trained observer. Permission to include another observer should be obtained from the client, providing the straightforward explanation that the new observer is learning clinical procedures. Agreement between observers should be 90% or better. The observer is now ready to serve as an independent or primary observer.

Recalibration

Many authors have recommended that observers periodically undergo a check of their observation skills during the course of a project to guard against "observer drift" (Foster & Cone, 1986). Observers occasionally can be cycled through the previous two steps for this purpose.

In conclusion, researchers and practitioners are encouraged to evaluate the effectiveness of this or any observer training program. In addition, research reports should include the results of such evaluations and a description of observer training procedures with sufficient detail for replication.

Validation of the BRS

Validation of an assessment device or procedure requires the demonstration of correspondence between scores on that device and some other accepted criterion of behavior. Discriminant validity is demonstrated when individuals meeting some criterion or undergoing specific training differ in their scores from those who do not meet the criterion or who have not been trained. In this instance, BRS scores should discriminate people who have undergone relaxation training from those who have not. Construct validity is demonstrated when scores on the assessment device are systematically related to other measures of the target behavior. In the present case, BRS scores should be related to other measures of relaxation such as self-report, physiological measures, or expert opinion. The BRS has been validated in both instances.

Discriminant Validity of the BRS

Schilling and Poppen (1983) trained groups of young adults who volunteered for a stress management program in three relaxation procedures—frontalis EMG biofeedback, progressive relaxation training, and BRT—and a music placebo. Everyone received seven training sessions as well as pre- and posttraining assessments, and all training was conducted in individual sessions. Biofeedback consisted of auditory feedback for changes in frontalis tension. Progressive relaxation training consisted of audiotaped tense-release exercise instructions from Bernstein and Borkovec (1973). BRT consisted of training in the specific postures of the BRS (see Chapter 3). Music consisted of taped presentations of music commercially marketed as a stress reduction aid along with attention-focusing instructions. Each of the three relaxation procedures resulted in statistically significant improvements in BRS scores, whereas the placebo procedure did not. These effects are seen in Figure 2.10. Direct instruction in the items of the BRS resulted in the greatest change, but statistically significant improvement also occurred for those receiving progressive relaxation and biofeedback. By contrast, people administered the placebo condition showed no systematic improvement on the BRS.

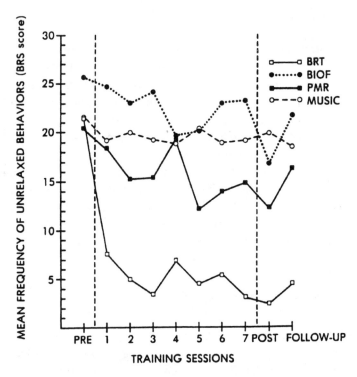

Figure 2.10: Mean Behavioral Relaxation Scale (BRS) (unrelaxed) Scores for Four Groups: Behavioral Relaxation Training (BRT), Frontalis Electromyography Biofeedback (BIOF), Progressive Relaxation (PMR), and Music Placebo (MUSIC)

SOURCE: Reprinted from *Journal of Behavior Therapy and Experimental Psychiatry*, 14, D. J. Schilling and R. Poppen, "Behavioral Relaxation Training and Assessment," pp. 99-107, 1983, with kind permission from Elsevier Science Ltd., The Boulevard, Langford Lane, Kidlington 0X5 1GB, United Kingdom.

Independent verification of this finding was reported by Norton et al. (1997). They compared two groups of college student participants who expressed interest in stress management. One group received two weekly sessions of audiotaped progressive relaxation training (Bernstein & Borkovec, 1973) along with a copy of the tape and instructions to practice daily. Those in a control group were instructed to "relax as best you know how." A variety of physiological and self-report measures were obtained before and after the training period. These researchers found a statistically significant improvement on the BRS, from less than 30% to approximately 40% relaxed, for the relaxation group, whereas no change occurred in the control group. By comparison, Schilling and Poppen (1983) found much higher relaxation scores before and after training than did Norton et al. (1997) (approximately from 78% to 87% relaxed for the progressive relaxation group).

Blanchard and colleagues (1986), as part of a hypertension treatment program, reported that patients receiving eight progressive relaxation training sessions achieved an average of 84% relaxed behaviors on the BRS for their last four training sessions. Unfortunately, neither pretreatment BRS measures nor BRS measures for patients in a thermal biofeedback group were collected. In a later report, this research group found that BRS scores steadily improved from about 70% to better than 80% over eight sessions of training in progressive relaxation (Wittrock et al., 1988). These figures are comparable with those of Schilling and Poppen (1983).

Luiselli (1980) described a Relaxation Checklist similar in many respects to the BRS. He reported that significant increases in relaxed behavior occurred on this checklist for college students who received a single progressive relaxation training session, whereas those receiving a control procedure showed no change.

Construct Validity

The BRS also has been validated by concurrent measures of relaxation. Schilling and Poppen (1983) found significant correlations between frontalis EMG levels and the BRS, particularly in the BRT and biofeedback groups. The BRS was not related to visceral measures of skin temperature or skin conductance. Norton et al. (1997) also found a significant correlation between frontalis EMG levels and the BRS across all participants. In addition, these researchers found significant correlations between the BRS and heart rate and respiration rate, even when the breathing item was removed from the BRS so as not to spuriously inflate the relationship. Their relaxation training and control groups did not differ on physiological measures; both improved over time. Wittrock et al. (1988) found a significant correlation between BRS scores and decreased systolic blood pressure in hypertensive patients during the last two sessions of relaxation training.

In a direct validation study, Poppen and Maurer (1982) measured EMG levels in the muscles anatomically related to the postures described in the BRS. Six male volunteers, ages 23 to 27 years, served as participants. EMG measurements were collected as the participants engaged in the relaxed or unrelaxed postures for 5-minute periods. Participants were not instructed to "tense" or "relax" but rather were instructed and guided into the postures as topographically described in the BRS. The mean EMG levels for nine muscle groups, as participants engaged in relaxed and unrelaxed postures, are shown in Figure 2.11. In all instances, EMG levels for relaxed postures were significantly lower than those for unrelaxed postures.

Tension levels in the forearm extensors are shown in the top left panel of Figure 2.11. Tension in this muscle group was equally elevated while participants extended or flexed their fingers. Similarly, tension in the forearm flexors, shown in the top middle panel of Figure 2.11, was elevated in both extended and flexed unrelaxed postures.

Tension levels for a unilateral sternocleidomastoid placement are shown in the top right panel of Figure 2.11. EMG levels while the head was rotated in a contralateral direction, to the side opposite the electrode placement, were greater than those during ipsilateral rotation.

Tension levels in the gracillis muscle group of the upper thigh are shown in the center left panel of Figure 2.11. Tension was higher when the feet were parallel, with the toes pointed up, than when the toes were pointed out at greater than 90°. The opposite was true for the vastus muscle group, shown in the center middle panel of Figure 2.11.

Tension levels in the trapezius were elevated when the shoulders were slightly raised, as shown in the center right panel of Figure 2.11.

Tension in the suprahyoid muscles of the throat, shown in the bottom left panel of Figure 2.11, was increased while participants engaged in 1-minute intervals of (a) talking, (b) coughing, (c) swallowing, (d) clearing their throats, and (e) humming.

Tension in the masseter muscle of the jaw, shown in the bottom middle panel of Figure 2.11, was elevated while participants (a) placed their lips and teeth together, and it increased even more while participants (b) engaged in smiling.

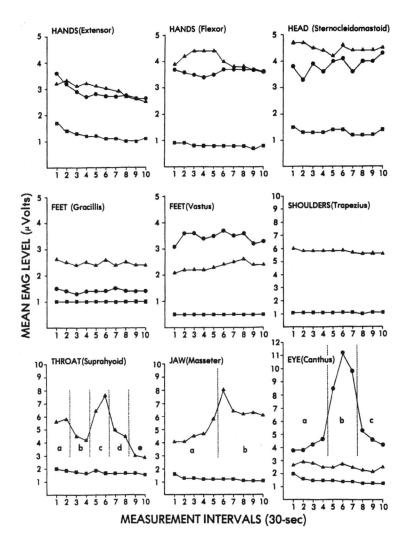

Figure 2.11: Mean Electromyography (EMG) Levels for Nine Muscle Groups in Either Relaxed (squares) or Unrelaxed (circles and triangles) Postures (see text for descriptions of postures and activities)

SOURCE: Reprinted from "Electromyographic Analysis of Relaxed Postures," by R. Poppen and J. Maurer, 1982, *Biofeedback and Self-Regulation, 7*, pp. 491-498. Copyright 1982 Plenum Publishing Corp. Used with permission.

Tension in the canthus area of the eye was elevated when the eyes were open, as shown by the triangles in the bottom right panel of

Figure 2.11. This figure also shows that tension increased even more when the eyelids were closed but (a) the eyelids were fluttering, (b) the eyelids were squeezed, and (c) the eyes were moving under the eyelids.

This study effectively dissected the BRS, showing that each item is intimately related to tension levels in particular muscle groups. Thus, when a person assumes a relaxed posture, tension in the associated muscle groups decreases markedly. As people undergo relaxation training (by whatever procedure) and learn to minimize tension throughout their bodies, this is reflected by the relaxed behaviors defined by the BRS.

The relationship between verbal self-reports and BRS is complicated by the fact that verbal reports of calmness often accompany a credible training procedure irrespective of other measures of relaxation. Schilling and Poppen (1983) found that participants in all groups—placebo or relaxation—reported increased subjective feelings of relaxation; these reports were not related to BRS scores or EMG levels. Likewise, Norton et al. (1997) found that both relaxation training and control groups improved to a similar extent on a number of verbal inventories including scales of state anxiety, state anger, stress, and arousal as well as the visual analog scale for relaxation. However, they also found that improvements on all these measures except "stress" were correlated with improvements on the BRS. Wittrock et al. (1988) did not calculate correlations between self-ratings of relaxation and the BRS, but their data indicate that both scores increased in a similar fashion over training sessions and that, like the BRS, self-ratings were correlated with blood pressure only in the last two sessions.

Summary

Predictive validity of the BRS was demonstrated by three separate research groups in which training in progressive relaxation resulted in improved BRS scores. More training appeared to produce more improvement, and no training or a placebo procedure resulted in no systematic change. One study also found that frontalis EMG biofeedback resulted in increased relaxed behavior on the BRS. According to the four-modality theory presented in Chapter 1, the BRS measures primarily motoric behavior, whereas progressive relaxation training and EMG biofeedback are primarily motoric procedures; thus, a strong association would be expected. If relaxation comprises a response class across modalities, then one would expect that training procedures emphasizing verbal, visceral, or observational modalities also would result in improved BRS scores. Demonstration of this relationship awaits further research.

Construct validity of the BRS has been shown by appropriate changes in concurrent measures of relaxation, particularly EMG levels. Tension in the relevant musculature is closely related to relaxed and unrelaxed postures as defined by the BRS. Correlations between the BRS and visceral measures of heart rate, respiration rate, and blood pressure have been reported, but correlation with skin temperature and skin conductance have not been found. Some relationship between BRS and self-report has been found, but self-report of relaxation often improves over time regardless of training procedure or other measures.

MULTIMODAL ASSESSMENT

As described in Chapter 1, relaxation is a complex behavior involving responses in the motoric, visceral, verbal, and observational behavior modalities. Relaxation training is assumed to produce behavior change in all these modes, and assessment of relaxation should reflect this complexity. Because there are no universally accepted assessment procedures for each of these modalities, the trainer will have to make his or her own judgments and selections. This section offers some guidelines in making those decisions.

Motoric Behavior

The BRS is an observational procedure providing a reliable, valid, quantified measure of the motoric aspects of relaxation. The BRS is easily learned and can be incorporated into clinical practice or research protocols with minimal disruption. It provides an ongoing measure of progress that is useful to both the trainer and trainee.

Unlike EMG and other physiological measures that are idiosyncratic to the particular electronic device employed, it provides a standardized metric, allowing easy communication between trainers and researchers in different settings.

EMG recording is a measure of motoric behavior that frequently is employed, usually in clinical and research settings that use EMG biofeedback. The frontalis EMG measure is the most widely employed and most widely criticized one (e.g., Qualls & Sheehan, 1981; Surwit & Keefe, 1978). There are questions concerning the relationship between frontalis tension and tension in other muscles and about its relationship to the client's symptoms. These same questions can be raised about any placement site. Also, the unit of EMG measurement (voltage) is not comparable across devices and is not easily understood by some trainees. Other difficulties with EMG recording include the expense of electronic equipment purchase and maintenance, the intrusiveness of wires and electrodes, the necessity to transform the data to some useful format, and the shortage of competent technicians.

Given the complications of EMG measurement and the availability of an alternative in the BRS, is there a place for EMG measurement in the assessment of relaxation? As a measure of overall generalized relaxation, the shortcomings of single-site EMG recording appear to outweigh its usefulness. However, in cases where the purpose of treatment is to reduce muscle tension in a particular body site or muscle group either through EMG biofeedback or some other technique, it is incumbent on the trainer to demonstrate that such changes actually occurred; that is, in cases where the presumed mechanism of action is muscle tension such as tension headache, temporomandibular joint dysfunction, or lower back pain, it is not sufficient to assume that decreases in pain reports accurately reflect change in muscle activity. Good practice, as well as a contribution to our basic knowledge of relaxation, requires that activity in the suspected muscle sites be measured and related to the treatment procedure. This will assure the trainer (and trainee) that the procedures employed are appropriate or, in negative instances, that some other site, treatment, or formulation of the problem is in order.

Visceral Behavior

Many of the difficulties with EMG recording apply similarly to measurements of visceral behavior. No single measure of autonomic activity will provide an index of the visceral component of relaxation, much less a measure of a global state. The expense, complexity, and intrusiveness of visceral measurement often exceed that of EMG recording. In addition, visceral measures are subject to many additional vagaries that limit their usefulness such as individual idiosyncrasies in arousal patterns, reactivity to external stimuli (e.g., noise, room temperature), and reactivity to other behavior (e.g., movement, respiration).

Nevertheless, when the goal of relaxation training is to effect a change in a particular visceral system, it is necessary to document that change. This applies to not only those cases in which the visceral behavior is the problem (e.g., hypertension, Raynaud's phenomenon) but also those cases in which it is the hypothesized mechanism of action (e.g., the vasomotor system in migraine, the respiratory system in panic attack). Gratuitous physiologizing may impress a naive client, but in the long run it does not advance the scientific status of relaxation training.

Verbal Behavior

The verbal component of relaxation is primarily a function of two factors, internal events and external social contingencies, with the latter often exerting the stronger control. Assessments involving verbal behavior typically assume the former and neglect the latter. Separation of these two classes of verbal behavior may be difficult and rarely has been attempted. Yet, to gather an accurate measure of relaxation, trainers need to consider both classes.

At the simplest level, different questions can be asked of the trainee to measure each verbal class. First, the trainee may be taught to discriminate these two verbal response classes by means of instructions. Trainees can be told directly that people often respond to questions about how they feel in terms of the situation and what they think their audience wants to hear. Examples can be given in which the reply to the question "How do you feel?" would differ depending on whether the questioner was a casual acquaintance, a doctor, a parent, or a television reporter. The trainee can be asked to describe his or her own examples to make sure he or she understands the concept of social contingency control. Then the trainee can be instructed to think of himself or herself as a private audience and to answer the question "How do you feel?" as accurately as possible. With this instructional history, relaxation can be assessed by asking the trainee, "How relaxed do you think your trainer wants you to say you are?" and "How relaxed do you tell yourself you are?" For each, a rating scale such as that in Appendix A may be useful. It also may be useful to administer a relaxation inventory, such as that of Crist et al. (1989) or of Smith et al. (1996), in terms of both the social and private audiences. By recognizing and accepting social contingencies in a matter-of-fact way, it may be possible to teach the trainee to make finer discriminations of private events and to report them more accurately.

Observational Behavior

Most relaxation training procedures ask the trainee to covertly engage in observation. Guided imagery, which targets this mode of behavior, attempts to measure it by asking the trainee to report whether or not he or she engaged in the requested behavior and to rate the "clarity" or "vividness" of the image achieved. Much more could be done. Assessment could include asking people to describe the imagined scene and scoring their descriptions according to the number and variety of details, perhaps analogous to a Rorschach protocol. Dadds, Bovbjerg, Redd, and Cutmore (1997) reviewed current research on imagery assessment.

A minimal level of observational behavior assessment entails asking the client to describe or rate the events that were observed while engaging in the relaxation procedure. For example, in biofeedback procedures, the client is asked to observe an external auditory or visual signal. This observation could be assessed by asking the client to describe the signal and the relation between it and his or her behavior. In progressive relaxation training, the client is asked to observe kinesthetic cues in the muscles and joints; in autogenic training, the client is asked to observe sensations of warmth, coolness, and heaviness in various body parts. Assessment consists of descriptions and ratings of the location, nature, and intensity of these events. Numerical scales and adjective lists could provide additional means for such assessments. Verbal report is necessarily the modality for assessing any covert observational behavior. Thus, the concerns about social contingency control of verbal behavior apply in this case as well.

Conclusions

Although relaxation training methods have been employed for centuries, the status of relaxation as a scientific variable is very recent. A major reason has been the lack of an objective measurement system for what is widely assumed to be a subjective state. Some professionals have learned to live with this state of affairs and have focused instead on measuring the relation between treatment procedure and symptom change, whereas others have made do with approximate measures of relaxation. This chapter proposes that measuring relaxation enhances the assessment of treatment outcome. The BRS was presented as an objective method for measuring the motoric component of relaxation along with evidence for its reliability and validity. This method is placed in the context of a multimodal conceptualization of relaxation. We regard the BRS as a crucial, but by no means complete, metric. It is available to stimulate further research on the assessment of relaxation and to aid in the development of more effective training procedures.

3

Behavioral Relaxation Training

T his chapter presents the standard Behavioral Relaxation Training
(BRT) procedure for use with adults and older children who have
"normal" learning capabilities. BRT is indicated for persons having
various stress, pain, or anxiety disorders for which relaxation, in a
generic sense, often is employed. As described in Chapter 1, BRT
shares many features in common with other relaxation training
procedures that make it useful as an intervention for the wide range
of problems for which relaxation is prescribed. In addition, BRT has
several features that may make it preferable to other training methods. First is the relative ease and rapidity of acquiring relaxed behaviors. Achieving proficiency and employing relaxation in everyday
situations takes additional time and practice, but trainees usually are
able to begin the process with a high level of success that sets the
stage for continuing progress. Variations of BRT, called "upright
relaxation" and "mini-relaxation" (described later in this chapter),

make it a highly portable and easily implemented skill for use in everyday situations. Compared to other training methods, BRT has several advantages. Unlike progressive relaxation training, BRT does not require muscle contraction, which may be contraindicated for problems related to muscle tension such as tension headache and myofacial pain. Unlike biofeedback, it does not require special electronic equipment. And unlike meditation and imagery procedures, it is easy for both trainer and trainee to monitor acquisition of target behavior. Chapter 5 provides more extensive comparisons of BRT and other relaxation training methods and describes in detail its clinical applications. BRT procedures for special populations are presented in Chapter 4. The present chapter describes some preconditions for BRT, gives a step-by-step explanation of the training method, describes some variations and extensions of BRT, and discusses problems that may arise in the course of BRT.

BEFORE TRAINING

BRT shares many elements in common with other relaxation methods. These include the setting in which training occurs, a general rationale for learning relaxation skills, and an expectation that the trainee will practice the skills. These common elements are discussed briefly in the following. The specific features of BRT are then described in more detail.

The Setting

The physical and social environments should be conducive to relaxation. As discussed in Chapter 1, for the trainee to observe the low-intensity events of interest, distracting and interrupting stimuli must be kept to a minimum. Lighting may be dimmed to provide a relaxing atmosphere, but it should be sufficient to allow observation of the trainee's behavior.

Full bodily support should be provided so that the trainee need not exert effort to maintain his or her posture. A padded reclining chair with footrest is routinely employed, but care should be taken that the trainee fits the chair comfortably. Small pillows can be used to fill gaps that may occur beneath the trainee's elbows or lower back. If training or practice is done on a flat surface such as a floor or bed, then pillows should be placed beneath the trainee's knees, forearms, and head, flexing the legs, arms, and spine slightly. This flattens the spine and prevents discomfort from lordosis. We have found a bean-bag chair to be useful for small children, and this also may be acceptable for adults. Seating position for the trainer, to allow adequate observation of the trainee's behavior, was described in Chapter 2.

The Rationale for BRT

The rationale provides reasons why the trainee should follow the trainer's instructions. As described in Chapter 1, these "rules for relaxation" state the relationships among antecedents, behaviors, and consequences of relaxation. The specifics of this generaformula are as varied as the individuals who are in need of relaxation training, and no universal prescription can be provided here. In general, however, the following steps are useful in developing and presenting a rationale: (a) review the problematic behavior, (b) present relaxation as an alternative, and (c) describe the training procedure.

First, the history and diagnosis process reveal that the trainee's current modes of responding are problematic. As discussed in Chapter 5, problem behaviors occur in any and all of the four behavior modalities. Complex emotional, pain, and stress behaviors are costly and ineffective ways of responding to life's demands. A review of these costs and discomforts with the trainee enhances the potential reinforcing value of relaxation as alternative behavior. In addition, there may be reinforcing consequences of the problematic behavior such as attention from others, monetary compensation, medication, and release from responsibilities (Fordyce, 1976; Goldiamond, 1974). The benefits of relaxation and other aspects of the treatment program must be presented to outweigh these consequences. The trainee's history also may reveal the antecedents of his or her symptoms—the social and physical environments that increase the likelihood of problematic behavior. These antecedent events provide clues as to the situations in which relaxation will be most useful.

Next, relaxation is proposed as a more effective alternative. Often a structural explanation is useful in which the physiological aspects of relaxation are described as overriding the problematic condition. Such explanations are variations of Wolpe's (1958) incompatibility or "reciprocal inhibition" hypothesis in which relaxation is held to be physically incompatible with the problem state, be it "anxiety," "stress," "arousal," "poor concentration," or whatever. A functional explanation also can be employed in which relaxed behavior is presented as effective in gaining desired outcomes. For example, by relaxing the eyes, jaw, and shoulders, a headache patient may reduce tension and prevent pain. Or, by sitting quietly and observing slow, regular breathing, a hyperactive child may do assignments more efficiently and gain the teacher's approval.

Whatever the mechanism, the rationale emphasizes the positive consequences of engaging in relaxation, although care should be taken not to imply a guaranteed benefit. No procedure has been found to be 100% effective, and the trainer should make an "educated guess" based on the literature on BRT and related techniques. Because progressive relaxation and electromyographic (EMG) biofeedback both emphasize the motoric modality, it is reasonable to predict at least similar success for BRT for problems on which data are lacking.

Finally, the training procedure, along with expected time and practice commitments, is described. BRT is presented as a motor skill in which proficiency comes with practice. Although the relaxed postures themselves usually are learned very quickly, beneficial outcomes result from regular practice and from implementation throughout the day.

Organization of Training Sessions

A typical BRT session takes about a half hour. Table 3.1 shows the recommended time intervals.

An initial adaptation period, in which the trainee is asked to sit quietly with his or her eyes closed, allows the trainee to "shift gears" from the previous activities of the day to the task of learning relaxation. Adaptation is particularly important if EMG or autonomic measures are to be recorded.

Table 3.1: Outline of Behavioral Relaxation Training Session Time Recommendations

Procedure	Time Required (minutes)
Adaptation	5-10
Pretraining observation	5
Acquisition (first session only)	15-20
Proficiency training	15-30
Posttraining observation	5

Pretraining baseline observations, described in Chapter 2, allow the trainer to judge the trainee's progress over successive training sessions. The trainee is asked to relax while the trainer scores the Behavioral Relaxation Scale (BRS) and collects a self-report at the conclusion of the period.

During acquisition, all 10 relaxed behaviors are trained through description, modeling, guidance, and feedback. Typically, for trainees without serious disabilities, this can be accomplished in a single session. Acquisition time varies, of course, depending on the trainee.

During proficiency training, the trainee practices the relaxed postures with feedback from the trainer. The feedback is primarily verbal, although modeling and guidance are used if necessary. The duration of a proficiency training session may be adjusted to meet the needs of the trainee. Some people, especially early in training, find it difficult to sit still for extended periods. This and other problems encountered in training are discussed in later sections.

The posttraining observation period provides a BRS score that, in comparison to the pretraining score, indicates progress in that session. It also provides a measure of relaxation over successive training sessions.

ACQUISITION TRAINING PROCEDURES

After presenting the rationale, answering questions, and gaining the cooperation of the trainee, the trainer is ready to commence. Initial acquisition involves four steps for each of the 10 behaviors listed in the BRS. These steps are as follows.

1. *Labeling.* Each behavior is given a one-word label by which it can be conveniently identified (i.e., body, shoulders, head, mouth, throat, hands, feet, breathing, quiet, eyes).

2. *Description and modeling.* Each relaxed behavior is described and demonstrated by the trainer. Commonly occurring unrelaxed behaviors also are demonstrated, and the contrast with relaxed behavior is drawn.

3. *Imitation.* The trainee is asked to demonstrate the relaxed posture.

4. *Feedback.* The trainee is praised for correct imitation. If he or she does not display the proper posture, then the trainer first provides corrective instructions. If after two or three such prompts the trainee still is unsuccessful, then manual guidance is gently employed to move the trainee into the correct position. When success is achieved, positive feedback is given.

As each behavior is successfully imitated, the trainee is asked to maintain the posture or activity for 30 to 60 seconds and to observe the feelings that occur. He or she also is asked to maintain the trained behaviors as each new one is added. In this way, all 10 behaviors are built up gradually. If the trainee should slip into an unrelaxed instance of a previously trained behavior, then this should be gently pointed out and corrected. If the trainee should become "stuck," unable to imitate or maintain a particular behavior after several prompts and manual guidance, then the trainer should move on to the next item. The trainer should reassure the trainee that one does not expect perfection right away and that success comes with practice. Other problems that may arise are dealt with later in this chapter.

Sequence for Training Relaxed Behaviors

The following sequence is recommended, although the order in which the relaxed behaviors are trained may be altered to meet the individual needs of the trainee.

Begin training with the relaxed *body* (see Chapter 2 and Figures 2.1-2.10 for descriptions and illustrations of the relaxed postures). The correct placement of the torso provides a foundation on which to build relaxed postures of the head and limbs. Next, train relaxed *head;* proper alignment of the head and torso also is a basic step that promotes relaxation in other areas of the body. Once body and head are correctly arranged, it is useful to follow a "top-to-bottom" strategy. This provides a convenient way for trainees to remember the relaxed postures when they practice on their own. An exception to this strategy occurs during the initial acquisition phase, when *eyes* are left open until all other behaviors have been trained so that the trainee can observe the modeling by the trainer. Thereafter, in proficiency and maintenance practice, *eyes* are relaxed after the *head.* Following the top-to-bottom sequence, *mouth* and *throat* are trained next, followed by *shoulders, hands,* and *feet.* Finally, *breathing* and *quiet* are introduced.

Adjustments to this sequence may be made if the trainee has difficulty with a particular item and it is useful to move on to others. It also is helpful to point out those relaxed behaviors that the trainee demonstrates "naturally," without training, to reinforce success at the start of training.

A Script for BRT Acquisition

The following is a suggested script for the initial acquisition session. The trainer should practice this to the point of familiarity, although rote memorization is not necessary. Language may be adapted to be appropriate for age, education, or cultural characteristics of the trainee.

Body

Labeling. There are 10 relaxed postures or activities. The first relaxed posture is called "body."

Description and modeling. Your body is relaxed when your chest and hips are aligned straight in the chair with no movement. [Demonstrate as shown in Figure 2.6A.] Your body is unrelaxed if your torso is crooked, if any part of your back or hips is lifted from the chair, or if there is movement in your torso. [Demonstrate as shown in Figure 2.6B.]

Imitation. Please relax your body.

Feedback. [Positive:] Good. Now take a few moments to notice the sensations as you relax your body. Notice how your spine is straight when your hips and chest are lined up. [Corrective:] You seem to be a little twisted to your left. Rotate your chest slightly to the right while keeping your hips still. [Guidance: Manual guidance of a person's torso may be difficult, and social conventions regarding touching a trainee's chest or hips should be considered.]

Head

Labeling. The next relaxed posture is termed "head."

Description and modeling. Your head is relaxed when it is resting on the cushion, facing straight in midline. [Demonstrate as shown in Figure 2.1A.] Your head is unrelaxed if it is tilted or turned to either side or tilted up or down. [Demonstrate as shown in Figures 2.1B-D.]

Imitation. Please relax your head.

Feedback. [Positive:] Good. Now just take a few moments to feel the sensations in your neck as you relax your head. Notice how your head is lined up with your body. [Corrective:] That's close, but your head is tilted a little to the right. Can you straighten it? [Guidance:] Your head still is tilted slightly. Is it okay if I adjust it so it is straight? [Be sure to ask the trainee before touching him or her to provide manual guidance. After correction or guidance, be sure to give positive feedback.]

Mouth

Labeling. The next relaxed posture is called "mouth."

Description and modeling. Your mouth is relaxed when your teeth are parted and your lips are open in the center like this. [Demonstrate as shown in Figure 2.3A.] Your mouth is unrelaxed if your upper and lower teeth are touching, if your lips are closed, or if you smile or lick your lips. [Demonstrate as shown in Figures 2.3B-C.]

Imitation. Okay, please show me how to relax your mouth.

Feedback. [Positive:] That's right. Now notice the feelings in your jaw and face as you relax your mouth. [Corrective:] Drop your jaw and let your lips open a little wider. [Guidance: Manual guidance usually is not applicable to mouth.]

Throat

Labeling. The next relaxed area is termed "throat."

Description and modeling. Your throat is relaxed when it is quiet and smooth. [Demonstrate as shown in Figure 2.4.] It is unrelaxed if there is any movement, muscle twitches, or swallowing. [Demonstrate.]

Imitation. Please demonstrate a relaxed throat.

Feedback. [Positive:] That's good. Notice the feelings in your neck and throat as you relax for the next few moments. [Corrective:] That's okay if you have to swallow occasionally, but then just go back to relaxing your throat. [Guidance: Manual guidance is not applicable to throat.]

Shoulders

Labeling. The next relaxed posture is termed "shoulders."

Description and modeling. Your shoulders are relaxed when they are resting against the chair and are sloped or rounded with the tops in a straight line. [Demonstrate as shown in Figure 2.5A.] They are unrelaxed if they are raised or twisted or if one shoulder is higher than the other. [Demonstrate as shown in Figures 2.5B-C.]

Imitation. All right, can you demonstrate relaxed shoulders?

Feedback. [Positive:] That's right. Now just relax and observe the feelings in your shoulders. [Corrective:] Your left shoulder appears a little higher than your right one. Lower your left shoulder a bit. [Guidance:] Your shoulders still appear a little crooked. Let me place them in a relaxed position. [Be sure to ask the trainee before touching him or her. Arrange the person's shoulders by gentle pressure to raise or lower them. Give positive feedback after correction or guidance.]

Hands

Labeling. The next area to relax is called "hands."

Description and modeling. Your hands are relaxed when you rest them on the arms of the chair, or in your lap, with the fingers slightly curled into a claw-like position like this. [Demonstrate as shown in Figure 2.7A.] Your hands are not relaxed if the fingers are flat or curled into a ball. [Demonstrate as shown in Figures 2.7B-C.]

Imitation. Please demonstrate relaxed hands.

Feedback. [Positive:] That's good. Now just continue to relax for a few moments and notice how your hands and arms feel in this position. [Corrective:] Not quite. Curl your fingers a little more so that a pencil could pass under your pinky. [Guidance:] That's still not quite it. Here, let me show you. [Again, be sure to inform the trainee before touching him or her. Mold the trainee's hand into the desired posture. After correction or guidance, be sure to give positive feedback.]

Feet

Labeling. The next posture is called "feet."

Description and modeling. Your feet are relaxed when both heels are resting on the footrest with the toes pointed away from each other like this. [Demonstrate as shown in Figure 2.8A.] Your feet are not relaxed if your toes are pointing straight up or turned outward too much or if your ankles are crossed. [Demonstrate as shown in Figures 2.8B-D.]

Imitation. Please show me relaxed feet.

Feedback. [Positive:] That's right. Just continue to relax your feet and notice the feelings in your feet and legs as you do so. [Corrective:] Your toes are pointing straight up too much. Just let your legs and feet flop apart. [Guidance:] Allow me to position your feet properly. [Ask the trainee before touching him or her. Place the feet in a "V" of about 90° with the heels a couple inches apart. After correction or guidance, be sure to give positive feedback.]

Quiet

Labeling. The next relaxed activity is called "quiet."

Description and modeling. You are quiet when you are not making any noise such as talking, loud sighs, or snores. [Demonstrate sounds.]

Imitation. All right, please demonstrate quiet for the next few moments.

Feedback. [Positive:] Good. Notice the relaxed feelings in your throat and chest as you quietly relax. [Corrective:] Please don't vocalize as you breathe out. [Guidance: Manual guidance is not applicable to quiet.]

Breathing

Labeling. The next relaxed activity is called "breathing."

Description and modeling. Your breathing is relaxed when it is slow and regular. [Demonstrate.] It is not relaxed if it is rapid or if there are interruptions such as coughing, yawning, sneezing, sniffing, vocalizations, or the like. [Note: The trainee is not told the specific number of breaths that serves as his or her criterion for relaxed breathing. In addition to the rate criterion, the trainer may wish to employ diaphragmatic breathing as described in a later section.]

Imitation. Please demonstrate relaxed breathing.

Feedback. [Observe the breathing rate for at least one 30-second period and compare it to the baseline rate. If the rate is less than baseline, then provide positive feedback; if it is equal to or greater than the baseline rate, then use correction or guidance.] [Positive:] That's good. Just continue to breathe slowly and regularly. [Corrective:] Please slow your breathing. [Guidance:] Please inhale slowly and deeply when I say "in" and exhale slowly when I say "out." [Pace the trainee's breathing so that it is slightly less than baseline rate. Provide positive feedback after correction or guidance.]

Eyes

Labeling. The final relaxed area is called "eyes."

Description and modeling. Your eyes are relaxed when the eyelids are closed and smooth. [Demonstrate as shown in Figure 2.2A.] Your eyes are not relaxed when they are tightly shut or if there is eye movement beneath the eyelids. [Demonstrate as shown in Figure 2.2B.]

Imitation. Please relax your eyes.

Feedback. [Positive:] That's right. Notice the relaxed feelings in your eyes and forehead as you relax for a few moments. [Corrective:] Your eyelids are closed a little too tightly. Allow them to become smooth. [Guidance: Manual guidance is not applicable to eyes.]

After completing all 10 items, the trainer should review them, as follows, to aid the trainee's recall. Be sure to pause for 5 to 10 seconds between each item and provide positive or corrective feedback as indicated.

> Now continue to relax while I briefly review the 10 areas. As I name each part, notice the feelings of relaxation. First, your body. Your body is resting comfortably with your spine in a straight line. Head: Your head is aligned with your body and supported by the cushions. Eyes: Your eyelids are gently closed and smooth. Mouth: Your lips and teeth are parted as your jaw drops into the relaxed position. Throat: Your throat is smooth and calm. Shoulders: Your shoulders are sloped and even. Hands: Your hands are resting on the armrest (your lap) with your fingers slightly curled. Feet: Your feet are resting on the footrest making a "V." Breathing: Your breathing is slow and regular. Quiet: You are relaxing calmly and quietly.

For most people, the initial acquisition procedure can be accomplished in approximately 15 to 20 minutes of the first training session.

Do not rush through the sequence, but allow the trainee to "feel" each of the postures when introduced as well as the behaviors previously trained. The trainer should observe all trained postures as he or she moves through the list; if an item should become unrelaxed, then the trainer should return to that posture before moving on. For example, when working on the hands or feet, the trainee may move the head or close the mouth. The trainer should point out the unrelaxed behavior and provide instruction or guidance as needed.

A brief review of the behaviors and their labels may be helpful at the beginning of the second session, as described previously, but generally no subsequent reviews are necessary. (More extensive acquisition training may be required for special populations, and this is described in Chapter 4.) After acquisition, the trainee moves into the proficiency procedure. Subsequent sessions begin with proficiency training.

PROFICIENCY TRAINING PROCEDURES

After all 10 items have been learned in acquisition, additional training is needed to reach the criterion on the BRS and to promote relaxed behaviors in other behavior modalities. Proficiency training involves instruction to the trainee, systematic observation of relaxed and unrelaxed behaviors, and verbal feedback concerning his or her behavior. Suggestions to observe the feelings of relaxation also are a part of training.

Instructions

The trainee is asked to relax all 10 areas. He or she is told to review the 10 items and to observe the relaxed feelings in each area. The trainee is told that the trainer will observe the relaxed and unrelaxed behaviors and periodically will provide feedback. Here is an example of proficiency instructions that may be used after acquisition is completed.

For the next 20 minutes, I would like you to relax all 10 of the areas that we have covered. Just to review, could you give me the names of the 10 areas? [Reinforce correct recitation and provide corrective feedback for any omissions or other errors.] While you are relaxing, I would like you to silently review each of the 10 areas and to pay attention to your posture and the sensations of each one. I will periodically observe your relaxation, and if I notice any areas that appear unrelaxed, I will say the names of those areas. For example, if I notice that your breathing is rapid or irregular and that one shoulder is higher than the other, I will say, "Breathing [pause] shoulders." You should then pay special attention to the named areas and relax them more. Do not be concerned if you feel the need to move, like to scratch an itch or swallow. Just do what you have to and then return to the relaxed position. For the last few minutes of the session, I will ask you to just continue relaxing on your own, but I will not provide any instructions or feedback. Do you have any questions? [Answer questions.] Fine. Now please sit back in the chair and relax all 10 parts of your body.

The Observation System

During proficiency training, the trainer systematically observes the trainee's behavior so as to provide feedback. A 2-minute interval observation program is recommended. This is frequent enough to prevent faulty habits from developing but not so frequent as to be intrusive. This program is similar to the observational system for relaxation assessment described in Chapter 2 but allows 1 minute to elapse between each observation interval.

Using the BRS Score Sheet, the trainer first counts the breathing rate for 30 seconds and then observes the other nine items for 15 seconds. The trainer provides feedback by reporting aloud the one-word label for any item noted to be unrelaxed during the observation period. If all items are relaxed, then the trainer should give positive feedback. After 1 minute passes with no observation or feedback, the process is repeated. If a denser schedule of feedback is desired, then observation and feedback can be provided every minute. Alternatively, a leaner schedule can be programmed by allowing more time to elapse between observation periods.

Feedback

The simplest feedback is to report the one-word label of any behavior observed to be unrelaxed. The trainee is instructed to attend to that particular area and relax it. If the label is not sufficient to prompt the trainee to correct an unrelaxed area, then corrective feedback can be employed. As in the acquisition phase, corrective feedback is a brief description of what the client is to do so as to meet the criterion for a particular behavior. Manual guidance usually is not employed during proficiency training. If a particular item is persistently unrelaxed, then more acquisition training may be given prior to the next proficiency session.

If all 10 items are relaxed, then the trainer should provide positive feedback such as "Good, you are doing very well." Some trainees respond better to positive feedback, and it should be included with the corrective feedback even though all 10 items are not relaxed. For example, a trainee may be told "Your breathing is nice and slow and even, but lower your left shoulder a bit."

An additional feedback procedure that is useful with some people involves showing the trainee his or her BRS score, from the posttraining observation period, at the conclusion of the session. This score can be calculated easily and quickly (the total number of relaxed behaviors times two gives the percentage relaxed for a 5-minute observation period). It can be verbalized as a numerical percentage, or it can be plotted on a graph to show progress over successive sessions. Care should be taken that this does not result in a competitive orientation by the trainee. Some trainees might want to know how they compare to other people or become concerned about "beating" their previous "scores."

After the first proficiency session, the trainer should ask the trainee for his or her reaction to the feedback. Was it frequent enough, or was it so frequent as to be intrusive? Was it helpful, or was it seen as criticism? The primary criterion for effective feedback is behavior change. The percentage of relaxed behaviors should increase and be maintained at a high level during the posttraining observation period. BRS scores of 90% or better typically are achieved within the first three training sessions. If this is not obtained, then the trainer may want to reevaluate the feedback procedure.

Directing the Trainee's
Observational Behavior

An important component of relaxation, as discussed in Chapter 1, is observational behavior. Along with instructions for motoric (relaxed postures) and visceral (breathing) behavior, the trainer should provide instructions to guide the trainee's observational behavior. The trainee observes both overt and covert events. The trainee observes (listens to) the trainer's voice providing feedback and is mindful of his or her own postures. But whereas the trainer observes the trainee's behavior visually, the trainee observes the kinesthetic and proprioceptive events that occur as he or she relaxes. In this way, correspondence between public and private events is taught. The trainer also may direct attention to other private events but has no independent means of verifying their occurrence.

A suggestion to observe one or two of the following events should be given every other minute in alternation with relaxation feedback. First are the public events associated with the relaxed behaviors. Trainees can be asked to notice their smooth eyelids, open jaw, sloped shoulders, straight alignment of head and torso, curled fingers, and "V" angle of their feet. Another set of events relates to feelings of heaviness in parts of the body and feelings of support provided by the chair. Trainees can be asked to observe the weight of their heads, torsos, arms, hands, and legs resting against the chair. They can be asked to attend to the feelings of support where their heads, shoulders, arms, buttocks, and legs come in contact with the chair. They also can be asked to observe the stimuli of the chair such as the softness of the cushion beneath their head and the smoothness of the surface beneath their fingers.

The stimuli associated with breathing also are useful for directing observational behavior. Trainees can be instructed to notice how tension in the chest and shoulders increases slightly as they inhale and tension decreases as they exhale. The temperature differences between cool air as it is inhaled and warm air as it is exhaled also can be observed. Diaphragmatic breathing, if employed, provides additional aspects of breathing to be observed.

Concluding a Session

After 15 to 20 minutes of proficiency training, the trainer should say quietly, "Just continue to relax on your own." At this point, the BRS is scored for a 5-minute observation period, as described in Chapter 2, during which time no feedback or other comments are provided. The BRS score may be quickly calculated and provided to the trainee at the end of the session.

At the conclusion of the observation period, the trainer should slowly arouse the trainee by saying very quietly, "Very slowly now, I would like you to open your eyes." A counting procedure is useful in which the trainer says quietly, "I am going to count to five; at the count of three please open your eyes, and at the count of five you may sit up very slowly and stretch." A pause of 1 second should occur between each count.

When the client is alert, the trainer should inquire as to the events observed by the trainee. Which events were salient and which were not? Were any observations particularly calming, and were any upsetting? (For example, one woman associated a suggestion of "heaviness in the legs" with concerns about being overweight—not a very calming observation.) In this way, an individualized list of relaxing observational behaviors can be constructed for each trainee and used in subsequent sessions.

Summary

A proficiency training session comprises several elements. The trainer should first make sure that the trainee understands the feedback system and answer any questions. The trainee is asked to relax the 10 items that have been trained. The trainer systematically observes the behaviors listed on the BRS for a 1-minute period and provides feedback at the end of each interval. Feedback may be in the form of the one-word label assigned to an unrelaxed behavior, a brief description of how to correct an unrelaxed behavior, or a positive statement noting the trainee's success. During alternate minutes, the trainer should direct the trainee's observational behavior to the sensations of relaxation such as feelings of heaviness, support, calmness, and peace. After 15 to 20 minutes of training, a 5-minute BRS scoring period is conducted, and then the trainee is slowly aroused. At the conclusion of a session, the trainer should inquire into the events observed by the trainee. A summary BRS score also may be provided to the trainee.

SOME PROBLEMS

On occasion, problems may crop up in the course of training. Some are common to other relaxation training methods, whereas others are specific to BRT.

One class of problems that has been reported in conjunction with both progressive relaxation training and meditation, and that sometimes occurs with BRT, has been termed "relaxation-induced anxiety" (Heide & Borkovec, 1983, 1984). As an aside, the accuracy of this term in describing the phenomenon can be questioned. First, "relaxation-induced" implies that the trainee first engages in relaxed behavior and that this, in turn, evokes unrelaxed behavior (Heide & Borkovec, 1984). Studies of the phenomenon have not indicated that any degree of relaxation occurs prior to the trainee's upset; instead, arousal occurs before training or right at the beginning. Second, "anxiety" implies a particular complex behavior that may not accurately describe the range of discomfort that various persons experience. For example, I have observed trainees report feelings of nausea or of falling; although discomforting, these are not properly labeled "anxiety." A more generally descriptive term would be "training-induced arousal."

Arousal rather than relaxation may occur in any of the four behavior modalities. Examples include motoric (increased EMG levels in particular sites, restlessness, sudden jerking, or "startle" response), verbal (statements of inability to relax, self-report of discomfort, anxiety, or arousal in the other modalities), visceral (shallow breathing, increased heart rate, nausea, vasoconstriction, or dilation), and observational (vertigo, dizziness, or attending to behavior in the other modalities).

How is the trainer to handle such reactions? No systematic data have been reported on treating these phenomena, but several avenues warrant further investigation. Heide and Borkovec (1984) suggested that persons who fear loss of control, abandonment, or social evaluation are especially susceptible to adverse reactions to relaxation training. They recommended that, in such cases, further analysis and treatment be directed to these fears. Where such reactions are relatively mild and occur early in training, simple reassurance and encouragement to continue training may be sufficient. If the difficulty persists, then increased attention to the particular response category may be helpful. For example, if the problem is vertigo, then the trainee can be asked to concentrate observation on the spatial location of his or her hands and feet or to open his eyes and fixate on an object in the environment. If the problem is muscle twitches, then the trainee can be instructed in exercises to stretch (not contract) the affected muscle group. Training can be shortened, either in duration or in the number of items covered, and gradually increased as the trainee progresses. Some people simply find it difficult to sit still for 20 minutes and require shaping from shorter to longer durations.

A problem that sometimes occurs with BRT is that a trainee may not be able to exhibit a posture because of physical limitations such as unequal leg length, arthritis, scoliosis, or other structural abnormalities. The trainer should be alert for such difficulties and make idiosyncratic adjustments in the relaxation criteria.

More commonly, a trainee may complain that a particular behavior is uncomfortable or does not "feel right" due to a habitual tense or asymmetrical posture. In this case, the trainee should be assured that the discomfort is due to the newness or "differentness" of the relaxed behavior and that, with practice, it will come to feel quite natural. I have observed that particularly with the head, shoulders, and body, objectively symmetrical postures initially may feel "out of line" to the trainee. For example, a person may be so accustomed to a slight turn of the head to the left that placing it in midline feels as though it were tilted to the right. With practice, such proprioceptive biases are easily corrected.

Another problem to which the trainer should be alerted is that some people begin to breathe through their mouths when they open them in the relaxed posture. This may result in drying of the oral cavity with consequent mouth closing and swallowing. The trainee should be reminded to continue to breathe through the nose; instructions to close the oral airway by gently placing the tongue on the roof of the mouth may be helpful.

In some instances, a trainee may feel that it is "impossible" to perform a particular item and express frustration at the feedback that it remains unrelaxed. For example, a person may feel unable to close the eyes without the eyelids twitching, to breathe at a slower rate, or to swallow less frequently. He or she should be reassured that the trainer does not expect 100% perfection. In addition, rather than negative feedback for unrelaxed behavior, the trainer can employ positive feedback for any instance in which the item does appear relaxed. Where difficulties persist, it may be helpful to combine BRT with other relaxation methods, as described in Chapter 5.

VARIATIONS OF BEHAVIORAL RELAXATION TRAINING

BRT may be supplemented in various ways to promote transfer to home and work situations and to enhance its effects. These variations allow the trainee to engage in relaxed behaviors throughout the day in situations that do not allow a recumbent position. They are, in effect, partial relaxation procedures and are not intended to serve as substitutes for full practice. They help to strengthen the trainee's discrimination of arousing events and provide calming alternative responses in those situations.

Upright Relaxation Training

An important aspect of relaxation is that it be portable. A central theme of this book is that relaxation is a skill that is usefully employed in a variety of arousing settings. Reclining chairs are not commonly available in most environments, nor is it possible to stretch out in full relaxed postures at work, at social gatherings, or while commuting. To enhance the transfer of relaxation to a wide variety of environments, a trainee may be taught to relax while seated in an upright chair. Such chairs are widely available—in offices, homes, waiting rooms, cars, and buses—offering ubiquitous opportunities to relax. Upright relaxation is an integral part of the mini-relaxation practice described in the following.

A study by Krmpotich (1986) measured tension levels of eight major muscle groups in six adults (three males and three females) as they assumed various postures while seated in an upright chair. From this and other research (Poppen, Hanson, & Ip, 1988), we have devised an Upright Relaxation Scale (URS) defining postures requiring the least muscle tension to sustain while seated in an upright position. After trainees have reached proficiency in relaxing while reclined, it is a simple matter to teach them the behaviors on the URS. The same procedures of modeling, prompting, and performance feedback employed in teaching the reclined behaviors are applicable in teaching the upright postures.

1. Back

Relaxed. The spine is perpendicular to the floor with the shoulder blades and the buttocks touching the back of the chair. A slight lordosis (concave lower back) is recommended.

Unrelaxed. The following is (are) observed: (a) bent forward so that shoulders are not in contact with chair back, (b) leaning back so that buttocks are not in contact with chair back, and/or (c) leaning to one side so that the spine is not perpendicular.

2. Head

Relaxed. The head is upright and motionless with the nose in midline with the body. A useful metaphor is to picture the head as a ball balanced on a stick (the spine).

Unrelaxed. The head is tilted forward, backward, or to one side.

3. Arms

Relaxed. Arms are bent approximately 120° at the elbow with the wrists resting on the thigh, approximately halfway between the hip and the knee. These dimensions may vary depending on the trainee's proportions. Proper placement of the arms ensures that the shoulders are even.

Unrelaxed. The following is (are) observed: (a) arms akimbo, (b) leaning forward on arms, (c) arms hanging at sides, and/or (d) movement of arms.

4. *Legs*

Relaxed. Legs straight and feet flat on the floor with approximately 90° angle at the knees and ankles.

Unrelaxed. The following is (are) observed: (a) legs crossed at knee or ankle, (b) legs extended so that knee angle is greater than 90° or legs tucked under chair so that knee angle is less than 90°, and/or (c) movement of legs or feet.

The following items are the same as defined on the reclined BRS:

5. *Eyes*

6. *Mouth*

7. *Throat*

8. *Hands*

9. *Quiet*

10. *Breathing*

The BRS Score Sheet may be used in the training and scoring of upright relaxation with "back" substituted for "body" and "arms" substituted for "shoulders."

Mini-Relaxation

As the trainee becomes proficient in relaxing in the reclining chair as evidenced by BRS scores, self-ratings, the Home Practice Form (Appendix D), and other measures, he or she can be introduced to the practice of mini-relaxation. In essence, this involves relaxing parts of the body while engaged in other activities. It is similar in concept to Jacobson's "differential relaxation." Daily activities that occur routinely should be reviewed with the trainee to determine how and where he or she can employ mini-relaxation. Rehearsal and role-playing of mini-relaxation in various situations can be incorporated into the training session.

Any of the behaviors defined on the BRS or URS may be relaxed in the everyday environment, depending on the other activities of the person. For example, mouth and throat can be relaxed in nonsocial situations in which the trainee does not have to speak or be concerned with his or her mouth hanging open. Breathing can be relaxed in situations not requiring speech or exertion. Hands can be relaxed in situations in which they are not required for manipulation. Shoulders and back should be relaxed while engaged in seated activities such as driving, typing, or other desk work. When a person is very actively engaged in a task, he or she should be encouraged to take periodic mini-relaxation breaks to literally "catch his or her breath" by closing the eyes, breathing slowly and evenly, opening the mouth, lowering the shoulders, and curling the fingers. Such breaks may last from a few seconds to a few minutes in duration.

The trainer should point out that the trainee can use regularly occurring environmental events as reminders to engage in mini-relaxation. Events such as hanging up the telephone after a call, completing a section of a book or newspaper, or stopping at a red light while driving can serve as mini-relaxation cues. For very busy people, a small dot of white typing correction fluid placed on the wristwatch crystal serves as a helpful prompt to take a mini-relaxation break.

Diaphragmatic Breathing

As discussed in Chapter 1, breathing is a visceral behavior, the control of which is an important aspect of many relaxation training procedures. Rate and pattern of breathing, as well as a person's observation of his or her own breathing, are subject to instructional control. Thus, a person may be instructed to breathe rapidly or slowly, deeply or shallowly, and to attend to his or her breathing.

Components of Diaphragmatic Breathing

One or more aspects of the following list of breathing maneuvers are characteristic of many relaxation and meditation training procedures (Bacon & Poppen, 1985; Boyer & Poppen, 1995; Fried, 1993):

1. *Abdominal breathing* in which the abdomen rises and falls while the upper chest remains relatively still
2. *Nasal breathing* in which air is inhaled and exhaled through the nose rather than the mouth
3. *Regular breathing* in which the rate and magnitude of inhale-exhale cycles is consistent over time
4. *Slow breathing* in which the rate is decreased from the nonrelaxed state
5. *Observation of breathing* in which the person is instructed, or instructs himself or herself, to concentrate on certain aspects of breathing

BRT involves Items 2 through 5 of this list, although only rate of breathing and gross disruptions such as coughing are objectively observed and scored.

Diaphragmatic breathing may have widespread effects on other visceral behavior, particularly vasomotor activity, although specific research on this issue is sparse (Bacon & Poppen, 1985; Boyer & Poppen, 1995). Diaphragmatic breathing may be useful for vascular-related disorders such as migraine, Raynaud's disease, and hypertension. It also may be helpful in disorders directly involving breathing such as asthma and panic attack. Fried (1993) proposed that "hypoxia" was a key feature of many stress disorders that could be remedied by diaphragmatic breathing.

Training in diaphragmatic breathing should begin only after proficiency has been achieved with BRT. Because trainees may achieve 90% or better relaxed behaviors on the BRS within as few as two sessions, diaphragmatic breathing may be incorporated into the BRT procedure very early.

Rationale for Diaphragmatic Breathing

The trainee should be provided with a rationale for the additional training procedure. Diaphragmatic breathing can be presented as an enhancement of relaxation that has specific effects on the problem for which the trainee is seeking treatment. As noted earlier, the literature on the direct effects of diaphragmatic breathing is sparse, so the trainer should not overstate the case. A statement to the following effect creates a positive but not unrealistic expectancy.

> Diaphragmatic breathing is based on methods that have been practiced for thousands of years for achieving calmness and reduction of tension. It involves learning to use the diaphragm, the band of muscle between the lungs and the stomach, rather than the shoulder and chest muscles to draw air into the lungs. This allows more efficient breathing with less muscular work. It allows you to relax the neck and shoulder muscles while breathing. [This may be helpful for tension-related disorders such as headache and myofacial pain dysfunction.] Diaphragmatic breathing may result in relaxation in the vascular system. [This may be helpful for vascular disorders such as migraine and hypertension.] It is incompatible with rapid, shallow breathing. [This may be helpful for panic attack, asthma, and stuttering.] And focusing one's attention on slow rhythmic breathing can have a general calming effect. [This may be helpful for anxiety disorders.]

Training Procedures for Diaphragmatic Breathing

Precise measurement of diaphragmatic and thoracic activity during breathing requires pneumographic or electronic strain-gauge equipment, which is beyond the means of most clinicians. Fortunately, it is possible for the trainee to place his or her hands so that both the trainee and the trainer can observe the relative motion of the chest and abdomen. The following procedure has been found to be consistent with measures provided by pneumographic recording (Bacon & Poppen, 1985).

While reclined in a relaxed posture, the trainee is instructed using the following steps.

Hand placement. Place your right hand on your stomach, between the bottom of your rib cage and your navel. [For most people, this is just above their belt lines.] Place your left hand on your chest, on your breast bone (sternum) just below your collar bone (clavicle).

Baseline breathing. Now just breathe regularly through your nose and notice the rise and fall of your hands as you breathe in (inhale) and breathe out (exhale). [Observe the trainee and point out the occurrence of diaphragmatic or chest (thoracic) breathing.]

Abdominal practice. As you breathe in (inhale), imagine your stomach to be a balloon that inflates, lifting your right hand. As you breathe out (exhale), the balloon deflates and your right hand falls. Your left hand remains still as your right hand rises and falls.

Feedback. Do not try to force it. Just attend to the motion of your hands and the feelings in your chest. Allow your right hand to rise and fall while your left hand remains still.

Some people find additional imagery to be helpful. The trainee can be instructed to imagine that his or her right hand is a boat, rising and falling on the slow, rolling waves of the ocean, while the left hand sits quietly at the dock.

The trainer should observe the motion of the trainee's hands for several breathing cycles. Some people are able to achieve the described pattern very quickly, whereas others have difficulty. Most are able to increase the amplitude of abdominal breathing, as shown by the motion of the right hand, but continue to breathe thoracically as well. If this is the case, then the trainer should comment approvingly on the abdominal changes but should not strongly disapprove of the thoracic component, only mentioning keeping the left hand still. A shaping process should be employed in which approval is given for one aspect of the breathing pattern and, with practice, the other aspect declines. The trainee may attempt to breathe deeply by raising and lowering his or her shoulders. The trainer should point this out and instruct the trainee to keep his or her shoulders still.

Slow breathing. Next, slow your breathing by pausing very briefly at the top and bottom of each breath, just a half second or so. Do not hold your breath or pause so that you are uncomfortable.

Additional practice and feedback. [The trainer should continue to praise positive aspects of the breathing pattern, with occasional corrective feedback for negative aspects.]

Tension release. Notice how there is a slight increase in tension as you breathe in and a decrease as you breathe out. Concentrate on the tension flowing out with each breath. Feel a slight increase in tension as you inhale, and then let go as you exhale. Each time you exhale, feel the tension leaving your body.

Combination with BRT. Now we are going to practice the diaphragmatic breathing and the relaxed postures together. Silently review the relaxed postures to yourself, leaving your hands on your chest and abdomen. Also notice the motion of your hands, the slight pauses in your breathing, and the release of tension each time you exhale. [Provide BRS feedback along with diaphragmatic feedback at 2-minute intervals, as described earlier, for 10 to 15 minutes. By placing the hands in this fashion, the criteria for hands and shoulders on the BRS may be disrupted; this should be disregarded for feedback and BRS scoring.]

Placement of hands at sides. [after one or two sessions with the trainee's hands on the chest and abdomen] This time, I would like you to place your hands on the arms of the chair (or in your lap). Continue to breathe diaphragmatically, with your abdomen rising and falling and your chest remaining still. Notice the sensations in your chest and abdomen as you breathe and let go of all tension as you exhale. [There may be some disruption of diaphragmatic breathing when the hand placement no longer provides feedback, but this usually is transitory.]

Some Difficulties

Trainees often report some difficulty or discomfort when they first try diaphragmatic breathing. It is foreign to their usual breathing patterns, and the awareness of and attempt to control a behavior that usually is automatic can be disconcerting. These facts should be pointed out to those who express difficulty, reassuring them that their experience is not abnormal. Like any new skill, such as riding a bicycle or swimming, there often is an initial period of awareness of awkwardness. But by consistent practice, most people can learn to become proficient and comfortable with this new style of breathing. Reassurance, encouragement, and positive feedback are sufficient to deal with problems.

In some cases, it may be helpful to take more time on each of the steps outlined rather than trying to accomplish all of them in one or two sessions. Also, it may be helpful to provide additional BRT sessions before introducing diaphragmatic breathing. When making the transition from hands on the stomach and chest to hands off, it often is helpful to allow the trainee to continue to use one hand, on either the chest or the abdomen, in an alternating fashion while placing the other at his or her side. The trainer should be careful not to blame the trainee for his or her difficulty and should take responsibility for the pace of training.

Home Practice

Relaxation requires practice if the trainee is to become proficient in the skill and reap the benefits of training. BRT is similar to other training procedures in this respect. There is consistent evidence that continued practice after the training regimen is an important factor in maintaining the long-term treatment effects (Blanchard & Andrasik, 1985; Reinking & Hutchings, 1981). The importance of home practice should be emphasized to the trainee.

The trainer should discuss with the trainee how to incorporate practice time into his or her daily routine. Homework assignments and time management counseling may be necessary to ensure the arrangement of distraction-free time and settings that allow 20 minutes of practice each day. The considerations presented earlier in this chapter concerning the relaxation setting apply to both the home and clinical environment. As the trainee becomes more proficient, practice of mini-relaxation should take place throughout the day. Relaxation in an upright chair and diaphragmatic breathing also are portable relaxation procedures that can be done for brief periods throughout the day, but these should not take the place of the daily relaxation period.

To help ensure home practice and provide data on trainee progress, use of the Home Practice Form (Appendix D) is recommended.

This provides a record of time practiced and self-reports of relaxed feelings. It also may help identify items that need additional training.

Conclusions

The variations described in this section have been employed by the author and his associates with clients having a variety of disorders. Controlled research has established some of the more immediate physiological results of these procedures such as reduced muscle tension and increased hand temperature. Clinical efficacy is based on less formal, unpublished case data. The procedures are consistent with the formulation of relaxation presented in this book as well as with much clinical practice, but further research is needed to establish their clinical utility.

4

Behavioral Relaxation Training With Special Populations

The emphasis on normalization and deinstitutionalization has accomplished much in teaching self-care and vocational skills to persons with handicaps. It is apparent that such individuals also could benefit from relaxation training (Calamari, Geist, & Shahbazian, 1987; Harvey, 1979; Liberman & Corrigan, 1993; Luiselli, 1980; McPhail & Chamove, 1989; Ortega, 1978; Reiss, 1982). For example, surveys indicate that persons with developmental disabilities suffer from a full range of emotional and behavioral problems and may actually be more susceptible to emotional disturbances than people without disabilities (Reiss, Levitan, & McNally, 1982). Persons with schizophrenia are particularly vulnerable to stressful life events (Liberman & Corrigan, 1993). The disruption and demands caused by relocation from an institution to a community living facility may be extremely stressful for people with various disabilities (Heller, 1982). Limitations in skills and opportunities also may be upsetting to persons with disabilities.

Despite such findings, treatment of stress-related and emotional disorders of persons with various disabilities has received relatively little professional attention (Liberman, 1986; Matson, 1985; Reiss, 1982; Reiss et al., 1982). Among the many factors responsible for this lack, the one relevant to this book concerns some difficult requirements of many relaxation training techniques.

Progressive relaxation, for example, requires a large degree of verbal instructional control, which may pose a problem for trainees with limited verbal skills. Meditation and autogenic training rely heavily on both verbal instruction by the trainer and verbal repetition by the trainee. At the other extreme, with biofeedback there is little that the trainer can specifically instruct the trainee to do to change the feedback signal. By contrast, Behavior Relaxation Training (BRT) requires little verbal instructional control beyond "Do this" accompanied by a modeled demonstration. An imitative learning repertoire is a very basic skill, which can be taught even to individuals functioning at low levels.

Progressive relaxation, meditation, autogenous training, and biofeedback all emphasize discriminations of covert proprioceptive and kinesthetic events, which in "normal" adults is accomplished through metaphor and reliance on an established repertoire of naming private events. For persons with disabilities, "concrete thinking" and a limited verbal repertoire make such discriminations particularly difficult to establish. In this regard, we have observed that many "special" people do the tensing exercises of progressive relaxation training easily but have difficulty with the release or relaxing part, ending up more tense than when they started. Lindsay and Baty (1986a) similarly reported that some clients with mental retardation treated tense-release exercises as a game and became more agitated and excited rather than less so. By contrast, BRT emphasizes overt relaxed postures and actions that are easy for both trainee and trainer to discriminate (Lindsay & Baty, 1986b). The "problem of privacy," in which the trainer does not have access to the internal events of the trainee, is avoided. Because the relaxed behaviors are publicly observable, immediate social or material consequences can be administered contingent on meeting specific criteria.

A related issue is the reliance on self-report as a dependent measure (see Chapter 2). Persons with disabilities may be particularly influenced by the social contingencies controlling either compliant or noncompliant verbal behavior. The use of the Behavioral Relaxation Scale (BRS) with BRT provides a useful alternative or supplement to self-report. Of course, the BRS can be used with any relaxation training procedure as a way in which to measure relaxation.

An additional problem with biofeedback is that the wires and hookup procedure may be particularly distracting and cumbersome for individuals with disabilities. The arousal generated by such devices may overshadow the relaxation task to be accomplished.

This chapter describes modifications of BRT that have been employed with adults having mental retardation, acquired brain injury, and schizophrenia and with children having hyperactivity disorder. Clinicians who work with "lower functioning" clients are encouraged to try these procedures. They also are urged to document carefully their observations and modifications of the procedure and to publish their findings so that this important area of application can grow.

MODIFICATIONS OF BEHAVIORAL RELAXATION TRAINING

All relaxation training procedures are adjusted to meet the needs of individual trainees. Even the most standardized procedures, such as Bernstein and Borkovec's (1973) version of progressive relaxation training, are modified for particular clinical or research protocols. This practice allows immediate gains in that a particular individual or group may be better served. However, in the long run, unless the modifications are carefully documented, this practice adds little to our knowledge base of which procedures work best in which circumstances and for which clients.

Each of the elements of BRT described in Chapter 3 is subject to modification so as to better accommodate special populations. These elements include the setting, the rationale, the procedure itself, the use of consequences, and maintenance procedures.

Antecedents of Training

Setting

The setting for BRT with a special trainee should follow the guidelines described in Chapter 3. Special care should be taken to make the training environment as distraction free as possible with respect to both intruding sounds from outside the room and visual stimuli within the room. It is a good idea to acclimate the trainee to the training room for a few sessions prior to commencing BRT, perhaps by using it as a place for review of various aspects of the trainee's program or just for "small talk."

Organization of Training Sessions

Care should be taken that the scheduled training time does not interfere with some favored activity of the trainee. Initial sessions should be scheduled at least once a day, more often if time permits. As acquisition occurs, sessions can be spaced out to two or three times weekly. The general training sequence outlined in Table 3.1 should be followed, but durations should be shorter, especially early in training.

Rationale

The trainee should be given an explanation for relaxation training according to his or her level of understanding. The purpose of training should be related to an area of benefit for the client such as "You can learn how to stop your headaches," "This can help you control your temper," or simply "This can help you feel better." Undue expectations should not be built up, but the idea of practice and improvement should be fostered. For example, a client may be told, "Relaxation won't make your headaches stop right away, but if you do this every day, they won't be so bad." People should not be summarily assigned to treatment but rather should be allowed to choose whether or not to participate and should be encouraged to ask questions.

Training Procedures

Acquisition Training

The same four steps described in Chapter 3—*labeling, modeling, imitation,* and *feedback*—are employed for each of the 10 behaviors on the BRS. However, the entire process is slowed, with deliberate shaping of longer durations and chaining of successive behaviors. Extrinsic consequences also may be added to the usual social reinforcers. It is especially helpful to begin training with those behaviors that already were relaxed during baseline so that the trainee can start off successfully.

A general strategy is to identify, label, and model the first item and request the trainee to imitate it for successive durations of 15, 30, and 60 seconds. The second behavior is trained in a similar fashion for 15, 30, and 60 seconds. The trainee is then asked to demonstrate both behaviors together for a 60-second period. The third behavior is then trained and imitated for 15, 30, and 60 seconds, and then all three are displayed for 60 seconds. In some cases, especially early in training for people who have difficulty even sitting still, we have found it helpful to count the seconds aloud. Also, the initial time requirements may be shortened for some trainees to as little as 5 seconds. This process continues until all 10 items have been trained. Corrective verbal feedback is provided immediately, contingent on any unrelaxed behavior occurring for an already trained item. The trainee is allowed 2 seconds to self-correct, and then further instruction or manual guidance is employed as appropriate. Praise is given on successful completion of each temporal criterion.

Typically, one to three items can be trained in each session. Each session starts with the trainee being told the labels of all behaviors trained up to that point and being asked to demonstrate all of them together for 60 seconds. Retraining of behaviors that do not meet the criterion should be done prior to proceeding with new ones.

Use of consequences. Token reinforcers, such as poker chips or coins, may be helpful for some trainees. This system can be part of an ongoing program in the training facility or can be set up especially for BRT. The details of the program should be worked out with the trainee and staff prior to training. Delivery of tokens should be concurrent with praise for meeting a behavioral criterion. Tokens can be dropped into a jar or can, making a clinking sound, so that the trainee does not have to watch for token delivery. Tokens also may be taken away for disruptive behavior during the session. Tokens should be exchanged for backup reinforcers immediately after the conclusion of the session. Extrinsic reinforcers such as soda, candy bars, or excursions also may be awarded after a session for compliance during the session. Using immediate reinforcers helps the special trainee stay motivated so that the long-term gains of relaxation can take effect.

Proficiency Training

After all 10 behaviors are trained in this fashion, the proficiency training procedure, described in Chapter 3, is employed with a few modifications. The duration of the training session may be shortened to 10 or 15 minutes. Corrective feedback rather than the one-word label often is necessary, and manual guidance may continue to be employed. Positive feedback for relaxed behavior is effective for special populations and should be interspersed frequently during training. If a token or other extrinsic reinforcement system was employed during acquisition, then it usually is desirable to fade it out during the proficiency phase. If tokens are continued, then they can be awarded at the end of the session on the basis of the BRS score obtained during the assessment period. Even without tokens, we have found graphic feedback, in the form of a histogram displaying the current BRS score and previous scores, presented after each session along with suitable praise is a good way in which to maintain interest and cooperation.

The proficiency criterion for special trainees may be set lower than that for other people. We have used both 80% and 90% relaxed behavior on the BRS for two successive sessions, with a minimum of six training sessions. The capabilities of individual trainees should be taken into account in setting a criterion, but the trainer should be careful not to underestimate their abilities and to be alert to ways in which to modify the program so as to improve success.

Maintenance Training

As with other trainees, special clients should be encouraged to practice on their own at times other than training sessions. In structured living facilities, practice time can be incorporated into their daily routine with unobtrusive checks by professional staff. High-functioning individuals can make use of the Home Practice Form (Appendix D) to monitor their own practice and progress. Mini-relaxation training often is appropriate for special clients. The goal of BRT for these trainees, as for any clients, is for relaxation behavior to be incorporated into their daily lives.

INTELLECTUAL DISABILITIES

A Pilot Project

McGimpsey (1982) first demonstrated that adults with mental retardation could be taught relaxation using BRT procedures. Her primary goal was to develop and test the feasibility of various BRT modifications described previously with members of this population.

Participants

Two men and two women (age range 21-44 years, Wechsler Adult Intelligence Scale [WAIS] IQ score range 67-79), who attended a sheltered workshop, were referred by their rehabilitation counselors. They were not diagnosed with particular stress or anxiety disorders, but their counselors judged that they could benefit from relaxation training. They were fully ambulatory and were not on psychotropic medication. Two of the trainees were married to each other.

Procedure

Training occurred daily except weekends. Sessions were 25 to 30 minutes in duration including 5-minute adaptation, 10-minute training, and 5-minute assessment periods. In addition to the BRS, frontalis and forearm flexor electromyographic (EMG) levels and self-report of relaxation measures were obtained in each session. A multiple-baseline-across-behaviors design was employed (Herson & Barlow, 1976) in which training was introduced sequentially across the 10 items of the BRS. This was replicated in the four trainees. Baseline, posttraining, and 4-week follow-up sessions consisted of 10-minute periods during which trainees were asked to sit quietly and relax but received no instruction or feedback, followed by 5-minute assessment periods.

During training, each new item was labeled and modeled for each trainee, followed by a request that he or she imitate the relaxed behavior for 15 and 30 seconds. Rehearsal trials, in which the trainee demonstrated the current item plus all previously trained behaviors, required a 60-second criterion. When all 10 items had been trained, proficiency training continued until the trainee demonstrated 90% or better BRS scores for two consecutive sessions. No formal home practice or maintenance procedures were implemented because training took place every day. Reliability of BRS scoring was established with a trained observer behind a one-way window. Reliability ranged from 88% to 94% agreement between trainer and observer.

Results

The results of BRT on each BRS item for each trainee is shown in Figure 4.1. This figure shows the BRS scored in a negative direction with decreases in unrelaxed behavior. In general, behaviors unrelaxed prior to training showed rapid improvement with the onset of training. Inspection of Figure 4.1 indicates that some behaviors were consistently unrelaxed prior to training (e.g., mouth, feet), whereas others were consistently relaxed (e.g., quiet, body). Breathing presented the most difficulty, perhaps in part because it was the last item trained and received the fewest trials. All 10 behaviors were trained within four to six sessions, with an additional two to five sessions necessary to reach the proficiency criterion of 90% (10% unrelaxed). There were some decrements in performance at the posttraining and follow-up sessions, although not to baseline levels.

EMG levels during the assessment period were not consistently related to BRS scores. One trainee showed a marked decrease in both frontalis and flexor EMG levels during BRT. A second trainee showed frontalis and flexor EMG increases over baseline at the start of training, which declined as training progressed. A third trainee

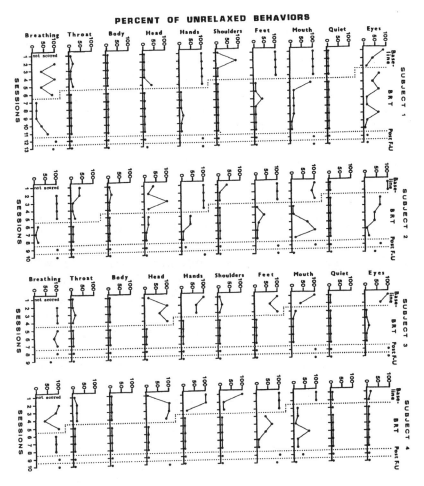

Figure 4.1: Percentage Unrelaxed Behavior for Each of 10 Items of the Behavioral Relaxation Scale for Four Adults With Developmental Disabilities
SOURCE: McGimpsey (1982).
NOTE: BRT = Behavioral Relaxation Training; F-U = follow-up.

showed a marked increase on the first day of proficiency training with a reduction to levels slightly below baseline thereafter. The fourth trainee showed a marked increase in flexor tension at the beginning of training with a subsequent decline, whereas frontalis levels remained steady throughout training. The EMG increases at the beginning of a training phase may indicate the trainees' reaction to a new task. With practice, these levels usually declined. At post-training and follow-up, frontalis EMG levels increased for three trainees, whereas flexor increased for the fourth.

Self-report measures for two trainees were consistent with their BRS and EMG scores, with improved feelings of relaxation as training progressed. Self-report scores for a third trainee fluctuated throughout training, both higher and lower than baseline. The fourth trainee did not like the procedure and reported feeling quite tense by the end of training.

Discussion

This study demonstrated the feasibility of BRT with developmentally disabled adults, who learned the relaxed behaviors in five to eight sessions. In some instances, BRT was associated with reductions in EMG levels and improvements in self-report. However, a number of limitations are apparent. The reasons for the individual differences in response to training are not obvious from this small N study. Another limitation was that the trainees were given no clear-cut rationale for participating other than that relaxation might help them feel better at work. Trainees who are motivated to alleviate some personally meaningful problems would be expected to show greater effects. Also, no maintenance procedures were employed, leading to decrements at follow-up.

BRT Compared to Progressive Relaxation

Lindsay and his colleagues conducted a series of studies comparing BRT to other relaxation and control procedures in adults with mental retardation. Following their initial observations (Lindsay & Baty, 1986a, 1986b, 1989), these investigators systematically compared BRT to progressive relaxation training and compared individual training to group training (Lindsay, Baty, Michie, & Richardson, 1989).

Participants

A total of 50 inpatients (25 men and 25 women) having moderate to severe mental retardation participated. They were judged to be extremely anxious and agitated, displaying restlessness and poor attention, with vocal and physical disruptive behaviors. Their ages ranged from 25 to 69 years (mean approximately 43), and their WAIS IQ scores ranged from 30 to 55 (mean approximately 44). They were randomly assigned to five groups with 5 men and 5 women in each group.

Procedure

There were four relaxation groups—two employing BRT (either group or individual training) and two employing progressive relaxation (either group or individual training)—as well as a no-treatment control group. Sessions were conducted daily except weekends for a total of 12 training sessions. Individual training lasted 30 to 45 minutes, whereas group sessions were twice as long. Assessments were carried out by raters blind to treatment conditions in sessions over 3-day periods prior to training, midway through training, and at the completion of training. The BRS was modified from its time-sampling format to a scale in which 9 items (excluding breathing) were rated on a 5-point scale with anchors of *completely relaxed* to *very anxious;* a 10th item was "general relaxation/tension." The 10 ratings were summed to obtain a score on a "behavioral anxiety scale." Reliability of this measure, within 1 scale point, was about 88% agreement. Pulse rates also were measured at the time of the behavioral rating.

Results

Statistical analysis (two-way analysis of variance with repeated measures over time) of the "anxiety" score indicated a significant effect of training, a significant effect of group assignment, and a significant interaction. All relaxation groups showed improvements over the course of training, whereas the no-treatment group showed no change. The individual BRT group had the greatest improvement, differing significantly from both progressive relaxation groups, and showed near maximal effects after only six training sessions. Group BRT training was midway between individual BRT and individual progressive relaxation training groups and did not differ statistically from either, although it was better than progressive relaxation training taught in a group format.

The pulse rate measure was more variable; there were no significant main effects, although a significant interaction was found. There was a trend toward a significant decrease in heart rate for the individual BRT group.

Discussion

Lindsay et al. (1989) concluded that group BRT was a cost-effective way of teaching relaxation to persons with moderate to severe mental retardation. They found BRT effects were achieved more rapidly than with progressive relaxation training and that participants had particular difficulty with the latter method in a group setting. This study did not measure the influence of relaxation on other areas of the clients' lives, but subsequent investigations examined the effects of BRT on other performance measures.

Effects of BRT on Intellectual Functioning

Lindsay and Morrison (1996) measured the performance of persons with intellectual disability on cognitive tasks hypothesized to be influenced negatively by anxious arousal.

Participants

A total of 20 adult inpatients (age and gender not specified), with WAIS IQ scores below 55, were selected because of problems related to agitation and anxiety such as pacing, vocal outbursts, and stereotyped mannerisms and verbalizations.

Procedure

Participants were randomly assigned to two groups of 10 each. Individuals in one group were given 12 sessions of BRT, whereas those in the control group sat in comfortable chairs for comparable periods and were read stories from a children's book. Immediately after each relaxation or story session, participants were tested on digit span, incidental learning, and general knowledge. The digit span test involved the oral presentation of series of one, two, three, and four numerals; any correct repetition was scored positively. The incidental learning task required participants to insert up to 10 colored pegs on a pegboard, changing direction (right, left, up, or down) after every third peg; participants were then asked to recall the colors of the last three pegs. The general knowledge test was based on a pool of 30 questions concerning common objects and daily routines. Performance from three sessions prior to training, Training Sessions 5 to 7, and Training Sessions 10 to 12 were compared for the two groups.

Results

Statistical analysis (two-way analysis of variance with repeated measures over time) showed that the BRT group steadily improved from baseline, to midtraining, to late training on both the digit span and incidental learning tasks, whereas the control group showed no change. On the general knowledge test, both groups were comparable with no change over time.

Discussion

Performance on digit recall and incidental learning was hypothesized to be related to short-term memory, which was impaired by anxiety and hence improved by relaxation. General knowlege was related to long-term storage and was not affected by anxiety or relaxation. Thus, laboratory measures of cognitive functioning were enhanced by BRT in persons with intellectual disability and anxiety. The authors recognized that no independent measure of anxiety was included; indeed, much of their speculation concerned hypothetical states and processes. In more behavioral terms, BRT, which focuses primarily on motoric behavior, was found to have beneficial effects on observational and verbal behavior. No measurement of relaxation was included; previous research (Lindsay et al., 1989) showed that BRT produced improvements on their behavioral anxiety scale, and one assumes that similar improvements occurred in the present study as well. Finally, the authors noted anecdotal evidence that persons trained in BRT were reported by ward staff to be less distractible and more engaged in other learning situations in their daily environments. These promising observations await more systematic investigation.

"Cue-Controlled" BRT and On-Task Behavior

The effects of BRT on performance during occupational therapy was examined to provide an indication of the usefulness of relaxation in the daily lives of persons with mental retardation (Lindsay, Fee, Michie, & Heap, 1994).

Participants

Three men and two women inpatients, ranging in age from 29 to 48 years, with WAIS IQ scores below 40 displayed a variety of agitation and anxiety symptoms such as shouting and other inappropriate vocalizations, pacing and other nondirected activity, and various facial and bodily mannerisms. Symptoms tended to increase when they were approached by other persons.

Procedure

A single-subject multiple-phase design was employed over a total of 30 sessions, conducted daily except weekends. All participants began with five baseline sessions in which they were simply asked to sit and relax. Two participants then received BRT for five sessions; on the sixth session, the cue words "quiet" and "still" were introduced and paired with the relaxed behaviors. Over the next eight sessions, the amount of BRT instruction and feedback was progressively reduced. The final phase was "cue only" in which the participants were given only the verbal cue and no BRT instruction. The other three participants began with a cue-only phase for five sessions. They then received a BRT instruction phase, BRT paired with the cue words, and a final cue-only phase. After each session, participants were provided with 20 minutes of simple occupational therapy tasks requiring color or shape matching and object manipulation. In addition, a new therapist was introduced at various times to determine whether relaxation effects were specific to the presence of a particular trainer or would be disrupted by the presence of a new person.

Participants were videotaped at the conclusion of each relaxation period and during occupational therapy. Independent raters scored the tapes according to the behavioral anxiety scale described earlier (Lindsay et al., 1989). Raters also measured the amount of time "on-task," defined as "meaningful manipulation of the occupational materials." High levels of interobserver agreement were reported for both measures.

Results

Anxiety ratings declined markedly only when BRT was introduced; there were no changes during baseline or when cue words were introduced prior to BRT. Ratings remained low or continued to decrease when the cue words were paired with BRT and remained at low levels for all participants during the final cue-only phase. Introduction of a new therapist, or the return of a previous one, had no disruptive effect on anxiety ratings. The amount of time spent on-task generally mirrored the anxiety ratings, remaining low during baseline and cue-only phases, increasing during the BRT and BRT plus cue word phases, and staying at high levels during the final cue-only phase.

Discussion

The authors concluded that the cue words by themselves had little "semantic effect" but could be linked to relaxation through pairing with BRT. Certainly, relaxed behaviors were maintained when BRT instruction was faded, but the role of the cue words in maintaining relaxation was not clearly demonstrated. This would require comparison to participants for whom BRT instruction was faded but no cue words were supplied. Individuals with normal intellectual functioning routinely maintain relaxed behavior in the absence of explicit cue words, although the role of covert self-instructions cannot be ruled out. It is likely that people with intellectual deficits may need external verbal prompts, or explicit training in self-instructions, to maintain a skill or use it in a new situation (Meichenbaum & Cameron, 1973). For example, self-instructions were found to increase on-task behavior in two mildly retarded children (Burgio, Whitman, & Johnson, 1980). Lindsay et al. (1994) did not mention whether they observed the participants using the cue words during relaxation practice or occupational therapy. Teaching the verbal component of relaxation would seem to be an important factor in the maintenance and transfer of relaxed behaviors in other modalities. Lundervold (1986) described teaching a mildly retarded woman to repeat the 10 labels of the relaxed behaviors to herself as a form of self-instruction, suggesting that this aided her in learning relaxation. Further research on relaxation self-instruction with this population is warranted.

BRT for Chronic Headache

There is a very sparse literature dealing with headache in people with intellectual disabilities. Given its high incidence in the "normal" population, one must conclude that headaches are underreported, either because of difficulties people with disabilities have in communicating their pain or because headache is less significant than other problems faced by those in this population. Michultka, Poppen, and Blanchard (1988) reported one of the few cases of headache intervention in a person with developmental disability.

Participant

A 29-year-old male with severe retardation (Stanford-Binet IQ score below 30), related to anoxia at birth, was a resident of a community group care home. He communicated with one- or two-word requests and could follow simple verbal commands, although instructional control was inconsistent. He had been diagnosed as having both classic migraine and tension headaches for 10 years. He had been taught to indicate the type of headache to staff members, who administered appropriate analgesic medication (aspirin and acetaminophen for tension, Fiornal for migraine).

Procedure

Training was conducted for a total of 20 sessions over a 4-month period. Regular scheduling was precluded by the client's frequent episodes of violent behavior, resulting in seclusion and canceled appointments. In an initial session, the participant was asked to relax for a 30-minute period. For the next 10 sessions, BRT acquisition training was administered as described earlier in this chapter, with the postures taught in a cumulative fashion having successive time requirements of 5, 10, 30, and 60 seconds for each. The client received verbal praise for his successes, and a break was taken midway through each session for a small glass of iced tea, a favorite treat. After learning all 10 items, he received nine proficiency training sessions; he demonstrated each of the relaxed behaviors sequentially and was then given the verbal cue "relax" as a signal to do all of them together. He was given periodic corrective feedback and verbal praise as he practiced. After he reached the criterion on proficiency training, a 3-month follow-up visit was scheduled. He was encouraged by staff to practice BRT on his own, but no formal records were kept.

The BRS was scored for three 5-minute intervals during the first baseline session and at the conclusion of each training session. Frequency of headache complaints and amount of medication consumption were recorded routinely by the house care staff. Headache and medication records were available for the 4 months preceding training and for 2 months following training. No records were available concerning his violent outbursts.

Results

Ten sessions were required for the client to cumulatively learn the 10 relaxed behaviors, and another nine sessions were needed to reach a criterion of at least 80% relaxed over three consecutive sessions. Acquisition training was slowed by the irregular schedule; the client often appeared to forget previously trained behavior after a lapse of several days or weeks. The client demonstrated 90% relaxed behaviors at a 3-month followup.

Monthly headache frequency averaged about 7 per month for the 4 months preceding training. Frequency increased to about 12 per month during the first 2 months of BRT and then fell precipitously to about 3 per month during the last 2 months of training, remaining at this level for 2 months following training. Medication consumption paralleled the headache frequency data. Informal follow-up at 3 months with a guardian with whom the client had gone to live revealed that headaches were very infrequent, and the use of Fiornal had been discontinued.

Discussion

Reduction of headache in this client followed his learning and practicing relaxed behaviors, although it is not possible to rule out other factors that may have contributed to this effect. It is unfortunate that data were not kept concerning the client's violent outbursts because these might have been related to his stress and headaches. Sessions occurred more regularly late in the proficiency training period; this is when the client made his greatest gains in BRS scores and experienced the greatest headache reduction. It is possible that BRT may have facilitated a reduction in outbursts, reducing the client's stress and headaches. McPhail and Chamove (1989) reported that progressive relaxation training was associated with a reduction in physical and verbal aggression in adults with mental and physical handicaps. Lundervold (1986) found that workshop staff, who were unaware that a mildly retarded woman was receiving BRT, reported that her aggressive outbursts and stress-related nausea had decreased. More systematic research into BRT effects on disruptive behavior and stress symptoms is needed.

Summary

Several studies have shown that persons with mental handicaps can learn relaxation skills by a variety of training methods (Calamari et al., 1987; McPhail & Chamove, 1989; Rickard, Thrasher, & Elkins, 1984). Research by Lindsay and colleagues suggested that BRT is particularly easy for such persons to learn and that BRT can be taught in a group format, a very efficient approach for facilities with staff limitations (Lindsay & Baty, 1986a, 1986b, 1989; Lindsay & Morrison, 1996; Lindsay et al., 1989, 1994). BRT has been associated with improvements in short-term memory tests and on-task behavior as well as with reduction of migraine and tension headaches. There are suggestions that BRT has positive effects on agitated, disruptive, and/or aggressive behavior, but further research is needed.

ACQUIRED BRAIN INJURY

Individuals suffering brain injuries incur a variety of symptoms including impulsivity, restlessness, motor impairments, and anxiety (Braunling-McMorrow, 1988; Lishman, 1973). Such problems suggest that relaxation may be a useful part of treatment.

Effects of BRT on Motor Tasks

Zahara (1983) demonstrated that persons with acquired brain injury could learn relaxation employing BRT. Taylor (1983) measured the effects of this training on various psychomotor tasks.

Participants

Three young men in a residential brain injury treatment facility were referred for relaxation training by their clinical team supervisors who reported them to be "nervous" or "irritable" and who felt relaxation would benefit their motor control, social interactions, and general health. Trainee 1, 22 years old, had been injured in an automobile accident 3 years earlier. He manifested both gross and fine motor skill impairments as in walking and writing. Trainee 2, 30 years old, had been injured in an industrial accident more than 3 years earlier. He displayed impulsivity, restlessness, and social skill deficits. Trainee 3, 29 years old, had been injured in a workplace explosion more than 1 year earlier. His problems included reasoning, memory, and speech impairments.

Procedure

Training sessions were scheduled three times weekly and lasted approximately 30 minutes including 5 minutes of adaptation, 15 minutes of relaxation, and 5 minutes of assessment. Motor skills assessment took place after each session.

A multiple-probe-across-subjects design was employed (Horner & Baer, 1978) in which baseline measurement sessions were conducted periodically for two clients while Trainee 1 received BRT. When Trainee 1 completed acquisition training, BRT was begun for

Trainee 2. Trainee 3 remained in baseline until Trainee 2 reached the acquisition criterion.

The acquisition and proficiency training procedures were similar to that described previously in this chapter. The training criterion was 80% relaxed behavior on the BRS in a 5-minute assessment period, after which six additional proficiency training sessions were administered. Posttraining and 3-week follow-up assessments were then conducted. Reliability of BRS scoring was determined by a trained observer in the training room, averaging 91% agreement. Frontalis EMG levels and self-report of relaxation also were assessed.

Two psychomotor tasks were conducted for all three trainees: a computer game and the placing and turning tests of the Minnesota Rate of Manipulation Test (MRMT). Performances on the computer game and MRMT were measured after alternate BRT sessions. Additional specific performance tasks were assessed for two trainees on alternate sessions. Trainee 1, who had difficulty writing and signing his name, was tested on a mark-making task while his forearm EMG levels were monitored. Trainee 3, who had speaking problems, was tested for duration of breath control while vocalizing vowel sounds.

Results

The trainees averaged about 25% relaxed behavior during baseline and showed no improvement over time. With BRT, they reached the 80% relaxation criterion in four to eight sessions and maintained or improved this level in subsequent proficiency sessions. BRS scores worsened at posttesting and follow-up but did not decline to baseline levels. Frontalis EMG levels showed no consistent change or relation to BRS scores. This may have been due to scar tissue and other damage related to the trainees' head injuries. Self-reports generally reflected an improvement in relaxed feelings during BRT.

No systematic change was observed on the computer game for any trainee. Performance on the MRMT improved for Trainees 1 and 3, but improvements during baseline for Trainee 3 suggest that this could have been a result of continued practice rather than BRT. Trainee 1 showed a large improvement in the mark-making task after BRT accompanied by a decrease in forearm EMG levels. His therapist reported that he showed much improvement in his everyday writing. Trainee 3 showed no change in vowel production duration during baseline but demonstrated a steady increase in duration after BRT began.

Discussion

This project showed the feasibility of BRT for persons with acquired brain injury. BRT was included as part of their clinical regimen to relieve general "nervousness" with additional specific clinical targets for two of the trainees (i.e., handwriting and speech). Trainees were encouraged to relax on their own, but no systematic effort was made to incorporate such practice into their daily routines. Participants were generally positive and cooperative in relaxation training but complained at times about the repeated psychomotor tests. Clinical target behaviors of interest and importance to the trainees showed benefits related to BRT.

BRT and EMG Biofeedback in Controlling Ataxic Tremor

Ataxia is a frequent result of acquired brain injury, impairing activities of daily living that require fine motor control. BRT, sometimes in conjunction with EMG biofeedback, has been shown to be effective in controlling tremor in the elderly (Chung, Poppen, & Lundervold, 1995; Lundervold, 1995; see Chapter 5). Guercio and associates reported its use with two young men with traumatic brain injuries (J. Guercio, personal communication, July 1997; Guercio, Chittum, & McMorrow, 1997; Guercio, Ferguson, & McMorrow, in press).

Participants

Trainee 4 was a 20-year-old male injured in an automobile accident 3 years earlier. He required a wheelchair for mobility and had difficulty with eating, drinking, and other activities of daily living due to tremor of his lower arms. Trainee 5 was a 21-year-old male injured 3 years earlier in a train collision. He had speech impairment and used a spellboard with difficulty because of arm tremor, resulting in frequent angry outbursts. Both resided in a brain injury rehabilitation facility.

Procedure

Sessions occurred twice weekly for each trainee and typically included several minutes of adaptation, 15-20 minutes of BRT, 5 minutes of posttraining assessment, and about 20 minutes of activity testing.

For Trainee 4, a multiphase reversal design was employed; the phases were baseline (5 sessions), BRT (6 sessions), BRT combined with biofeedback (11 sessions), return to baseline (5 sessions), and return to combined BRT-biofeedback (5 sessions). A 1-year follow-up assessment employed combined BRT-biofeedback. During combined BRT-biofeedback, relaxation instructions continued and an auditory signal indicating activity in the flexors and extensors of the forearm of the trainee's dominant side was provided to decrease tension. Immediately following each relaxation period, he was raised to an upright position and performed eating and drinking tasks. During eating, he took a spoonful of dry cereal from a bowl and transferred it to his mouth. During drinking, he grasped a cup of water (two thirds full), moved it to his lips, and moved it back to the table. (He did not actually consume the cereal or water during the tests.) Each movement was performed three times. Forearm EMG biofeedback was provided for eating and drinking tasks during the combined BRT-biofeedback phases.

For Trainee 5, a changing criterion design (Hartman & Hall, 1976) was employed based on forearm EMG levels during activity training. He received three baseline sessions and a total of 20 BRT sessions. After each relaxation period, he was provided with his spellboard and instructed to spell "My name is Boe" for three consecutive trials. After eight BRT sessions, he was provided with an auditory signal that sounded when his forearm EMG levels exceeded a threshold value while performing the spellboard task. The threshold criterion was decreased in three successive stages.

Measurement for both participants included the BRS, scored for 5 minutes at the conclusion of relaxation, and forearm EMG levels measured during activity testing. In addition, forearm EMG levels were measured during relaxation for Trainee 4, and the Clinical Rating of Tremor Scale (CRTS) (Fahn, Tolosa, & Marin, 1988) was scored for Trainee 5 during spellboard activity.

Results

For Trainee 4, BRS scores and forearm EMG levels during relaxation generally were inversely related, although there were some inconsistencies. During the initial baseline, BRS scores were very poor, although EMG levels were fairly low. During BRT, BRS scores improved to above 90% relaxed, whereas EMG levels fell to their lowest points. EMG levels during eating and drinking tasks were very much higher than while the client relaxed, as expected. Nonetheless, EMG levels during activity showed a marked reduction when BRT was implemented. In the combined BRT-biofeedback phase, BRS scores worsened somewhat, to about 85% relaxed, and EMG levels increased slightly. EMG levels during eating and drinking activities did not change when biofeedback was added. During return to baseline, BRS scores declined (although not to initial baseline levels), relaxed EMG values increased to above the initial baseline, and activity EMG values increased markedly to baseline levels. During return to combined BRT-biofeedback, BRS scores improved to their previous level, relaxed EMG values remained fairly high, and activity EMG values improved. At follow-up, BRS was above 90%, relaxed EMG values were at a very low level, and activity EMG values were at a reduced level.

For Trainee 5, BRS scores also improved immediately when BRT was begun, although not to the level of Trainee 4. His BRS scores continued to improve and were consistently above 80% after 15 sessions. EMG levels during the spellboard task decreased steadily with BRT and were consistent with changes in the biofeedback criteria, concluding with values about half his baseline levels. Clinical tremor ratings also improved immediately with BRT and showed continued improvement with training. Beginning at "extreme" levels during baseline, CRTS scores improved to the "mild" range by the end of training.

Discussion

Previous research has shown that forearm EMG levels are closely related to other indexes of tremor (Chung et al., 1995; Lundervold, 1995; see Chapter 5). Interventions that decrease EMG levels often have the effect of decreasing tremor and improving function.

Both clients showed an immediate decrease in forearm EMG levels during activity tests when BRT was implemented. Trainee 5 continued to improve with training and appeared to show an added effect of EMG biofeedback, whereas Trainee 4 did not. Systematic rating of tremor indicated progressive improvements for Trainee 5. Informal observation by direct care staff suggested that eating skills and object manipulation were improved for Trainee 4. No measures outside the therapy situation were obtained. Systematic measurement of relaxation effects on activities of daily living is needed in future research. The decrement in performance during the return to baseline phase for Trainee 4 indicates that this client continued to depend on therapist feedback. Because the goal of BRT is independent performance of relaxation skills, specific training in self-management appears to be needed, perhaps through the use of cue words or self-instruction.

HYPERACTIVITY DISORDER

Hyperactivity is conservatively estimated to occur in 3% to 5% of American schoolchildren, predominantly in boys (Barkley, 1981). Children with hyperactivity are characterized as impulsive, overactive, incapable of sustained attention, socially disruptive, and poor students. Stimulant medication, which has a "paradoxical" calming effect in many children, is by far the most common treatment. Long-term drug use has raised serious objections because of growth retardation, somatic side effects, and lack of academic progress in medicated children (O'Leary, 1980; Werry & Sprague, 1974; Whalen & Henker, 1976).

Relaxation training has been proposed as a possible behavioral alternative to drugs. Raymer and Poppen (1985) reviewed several studies that reported positive effects of frontalis EMG biofeedback or progressive relaxation on measures such as parent rating scales, psychological tests, and academic and psychomotor tasks. Other research found relaxation training to be no more effective than attention control procedures in improving performance.

Teaching BRT to Boys With Hyperactivity

Raymer contributed to the BRT modifications described at the beginning of this chapter by adapting the procedure for use with children having hyperactivity disorder (Raymer & Poppen, 1985). His study showed the feasibility of using BRT with this population and demonstrated some benefits that may result.

Participants

Trainee 1, 11 years old, lived in a group home because of family problems with his behavior; he was taking 10 milligrams of Ritalin daily at the start of the study. Trainee 2, 9 years old, was referred by his physician; Ritalin had not improved his behavior, and his parents were reluctant to reinstate drug treatment. Trainee 3, 9 years old, was referred by his school because of poor performance; he had a history of taking Ritalin, but his parents objected to his continuing its use. All boys met the diagnostic criteria of Barkley (1981) and had been diagnosed as hyperactive by at least one physician.

Procedure

EMG monitoring equipment was first demonstrated to the boys and then kept out of sight by draping with sheets. Reliability observations, for at least 25% of the sessions with each child, were made through a one-way window by a trained observer in an adjacent room. Agreement between observer and trainer was better than 90% for each child.

Training sessions were conducted approximately twice a week. A multiple-probe-across-subjects design was employed, similar to that employed by Zahara (1983) and Taylor (1983) described previously. Measures included the BRS, frontalis EMG levels, parent ratings on the Hyperactivity Index of the Conners Questionnaire (Goyette, Conners, & Ulrich, 1978), and self-report in which the boys were asked, "Answer yes or no: Do you feel relaxed?"

Training followed the format described at the beginning of this chapter. Tokens (poker chips) initially were delivered for approximations to relaxed behaviors such as lying in the recliner and listening to the trainer. Later they were contingent on performance of relaxed behaviors for specified periods of time. Tokens were spent after each session on an outing, treat, or trinket provided by the trainer.

After reaching the acquisition criterion, Trainee 1 had difficulty meeting the proficiency criterion. During an outing, the trainer noticed that the child sat quietly in a beanbag chair. Reasoning that the beanbag provided better body support than the big recliner, a beanbag was employed in the next session with an immediate improvement in relaxed behaviors. After the child reached the proficiency criterion, a reversal to the recliner was conducted and then back to the beanbag. The same procedure was followed for Trainees 2 and 3.

Follow-up measurements were conducted 2 to 3 months after training, at which time the parents were offered the opportunity to learn the procedure in their homes. All parents agreed to the program, including purchasing beanbag chairs and implementing token reinforcement. For each trainee, the trainer first conducted an initial home baseline session. Next, the mother was trained briefly in the relaxed behaviors herself and observed the trainer conduct BRT and BRS scoring with her child. During the third and fourth sessions, the mother conducted BRT, following prompts provided by the trainer. Thereafter, the mother conducted BRT for 10 consecutive days with the trainer observing on the 1st, 5th, and 10th days. A final follow-up measurement session was conducted in the home a month later.

Results

BRS scores for all three boys are shown in Figure 4.2. They displayed low variable rates of relaxed behaviors at baseline with no improvement. Scores increased with the onset of BRT, but plateaus were reached between 40% and 70% relaxed. Introduction of the beanbag chair resulted in rapid achievement of the proficiency criterion (80% or better for two consecutive sessions) for all boys. A reversal session in the recliner disrupted BRS scores, but they rapidly recovered when the beanbag was reinstated. Some decrement at 1-month follow-up was noted, particularly for Trainee 1, who was given a second session in which he was instructed to "relax like you were taught," resulting in immediate improvement.

Decreases in BRS scores occurred for all three boys in the initial home baseline sessions. Performance improved immediately with training by the mothers and was maintained at the last follow-up.

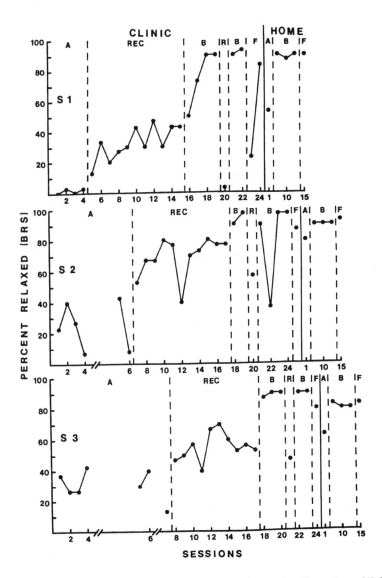

Figure 4.2: Behavioral Relaxation Scale (BRS) Scores for Three Boys With Hyperactivity Disorder

SOURCE: Reprinted from *Journal of Behavior Therapy and Experimental Psychiatry, 16*, R. H. Raymer and R. Poppen, "Behavioral Relaxation Training With Hyperactive Children," 1985, pp. 309-316, with kind permission from Elsevier Science Ltd., The Boulevard, Langford Lane, Kidlington 0X5 1GB, United Kingdom.

NOTE: A = baseline; REC = recliner training; B = beanbag chair training; R = reversal to recliner; F = follow-up.

Frontalis EMG data for each child showed a strong correspondence to the BRS scores, as shown in Figure 4.3. For Trainees 1 and 2, there was a steady improvement during BRT in the recliner with no large change when the beanbag was introduced. For Trainee 3, EMG levels improved only slightly until the beanbag was implemented. Reversal effects are obvious for all three boys. EMG levels increased markedly during the home baseline sessions but declined rapidly when mothers implemented BRT and were maintained at low levels at follow-up. Correlations between BRS scores and EMG levels were $-.42$ ($p < .05$) for Trainee 1, $-.56$ ($p < .01$) for Trainee 2, and $-.81$ ($p < .001$) for Trainee 3. (The negative correlations indicate that increases in relaxed behavior were associated with decreases in EMG levels.)

Parent ratings on the Hyperactivity Index of the Conners Questionnaire are shown in Figure 4.4. There was no systematic improvement during baseline. During BRT, there was a gradual improvement in ratings with scores at the first follow-up about 1 standard deviation lower than those at the end of baseline. However, these scores still were within the "hyperactive" range. Scores for all three children improved markedly immediately on home training by the mothers. All were within the "normal" range at the final home follow-up.

In addition to these formal measures, the parents were asked about their reactions to the procedures. All reported that it was convenient and easily implemented and that they felt it had benefited their children. They reported things such as a child employing the procedures on his own while watching television or showing off his skill for relatives.

All children reported that they felt relaxed on every session including baseline. This was taken as an indication that their verbal reports were related to the social contingencies rather than to their feelings of relaxation.

Discussion

This project demonstrated that children meeting multiple diagnostic criteria for hyperactivity could learn to relax, as measured by both the BRS and frontalis EMG levels. A beanbag chair proved to be an important factor, underscoring the need to provide full body support. Progress may have been quicker had a beanbag been provided from the beginning. Maintenance of relaxed behavior was

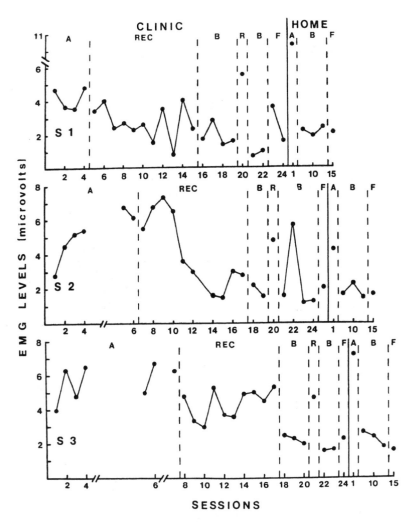

Figure 4.3: Frontalis Electromyographic (EMG) Levels for Three Boys With Hyperactivity Disorder

SOURCE: Reprinted from *Journal of Behavior Therapy and Experimental Psychiatry*, 16, R. H. Raymer and R. Poppen, "Behavioral Relaxation Training With Hyperactive Children," 1985, pp. 309-316, with kind permission from Elsevier Science Ltd., The Boulevard, Langford Lane, Kidlington 0X5 1GB, United Kingdom.
NOTE: Phases are as designated in Figure 4.2.

generally very good, with decrements in performance easily remedied by instructions or brief training. Effects of relaxation on the

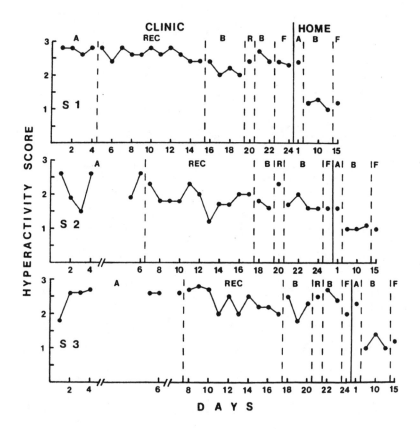

Figure 4.4: Parents' Hyperactivity Index Ratings for Three Boys With Hyperactivity Disorder

SOURCE: Reprinted from *Journal of Behavior Therapy and Experimental Psychiatry, 16*, R. H. Raymer and R. Poppen, "Behavioral Relaxation Training With Hyperactive Children," 1985, pp. 309-316, with kind permission from Elsevier Science Ltd., The Boulevard, Langford Lane, Kidlington 0X5 1GB, United Kingdom.

NOTE: Phases are as designated in Figure 4.2.

broader class of hyperactive behaviors were reflected in improvements on the Hyperactivity Index of the Conners Questionnaire. Although no formal efforts were made to transfer the skills to the home environment during the office training phase, some improvements on the Hyperactivity Index were reported by all parents. When home practice was implemented, marked improvements on the Hyperactivity Index were noted. This may reflect actual changes in the children's comportment at home due to relaxation, or it may have altered the parents' perception of their children. Objective observation of child behavior in the home would be needed to address this question.

Teaching Parents to Teach BRT to Their Children

In the preceding study, parents learned to administer BRT very easily, although at the time the children were already quite proficient in the relaxed behaviors. Donney undertook to teach parents to conduct BRT in their own homes right from the beginning (Donney & Poppen, 1989). This avoided the problem of transferring training to the home environment and demonstrated how easily a nonprofessional could learn to do BRT.

Participants

Three boys were referred by their pediatricians, who judged them to be inadequately controlled by medication. Trainee 1, 8 years old, was taking 25 milligrams of Ritalin daily. Trainee 2, 10 years old, was taking 20 milligrams of Ritalin daily. Trainee 3, 9 years old, was taking 15 milligrams of Ritalin daily. In addition to the medical diagnosis, the boys met the criteria described in Barkley (1981). Two families purchased beanbag chairs, and one was provided for the third. The mothers of Trainees 1 and 2, and the father of Trainee 3, participated in training their children.

Procedure

Training and observation were conducted in each child's room or the family living room with efforts made to minimize distractions. A simple A-B design (baseline-training) with follow-up was employed, replicated across the three children, because time limitations prohibited the more elaborate multiple-baseline approach. Training took place during the summer school vacation months. Sessions were scheduled twice weekly, depending on the commitments of trainer and parents. Each child's training program suffered one or more lengthy interruptions due to vacations or illnesses.

Measures included the BRS, frontalis EMG levels, and parent ratings on the Hyperactivity Index of the Conners Questionnaire (Goyette et al., 1978). Prior to training and at follow-up, the Home Situations Questionnaire (Barkley, 1981) was filled out by the parents and the School Situations Questionnaire (Barkley, 1981) was filled out by the boys' schoolteachers. Classroom observations were conducted for Trainee 2 on three behaviors ("out of seat," "talking out," and "on-task") by a teacher's assistant during baseline and by the trainer after treatment because the assistant no longer was available. On 25% of the sessions, another trained observer accompanied the trainer to measure reliability of the BRS.

For each trainee, four baseline sessions were conducted with the trainer and parent both present. The child was asked to sit quietly for 20 minutes; the last 5 minutes comprised the measurement period for scoring the BRS and recording EMG levels. After each baseline session, the trainer and parent discussed the BRS scoring. The parent was given a copy of the BRS definitions and practiced the relaxed behaviors himself or herself while the trainer provided feedback, guidance, and praise. Next, the trainer modeled relaxed and unrelaxed behaviors while the parent provided feedback.

Training sessions consisted of 5 minutes of adaptation, 20 minutes of BRT, and 5 minutes of assessment. The first three behaviors were taught by the trainer, whereas the parent observed and scored during the assessment period. Training was conducted as described earlier in this chapter, including delivery of tokens for successful behavior. The trainer and parent reviewed their BRS Score Sheets after each session, and corrective feedback was given for discrepancies. The next two behaviors were taught by the parent, guided by silent signals from the trainer. The trainer kept track of the observation schedule and indicated to the parent which behaviors were unrelaxed by pointing to her own body. The last five behaviors were taught by the parent alone with the trainer providing corrective feedback after the session if needed.

After all 10 items had been completed, proficiency training was conducted by the parent to a criterion of two successive sessions of 80% relaxed behaviors during the assessment period. The trainer's role at this point was to conduct BRS and EMG assessments and to provide feedback and encouragement. Tokens were spent by the child as soon after the session as possible on small treats and outings delivered by the parents. Throughout training, the families were encouraged to practice on their own, although no systematic data were collected. Two follow-up assessment sessions were conducted at 1 and 3 months.

Results

Figure 4.5 shows the BRS scores for these children. There was no improvement during baseline; if anything, performance worsened. When BRT was implemented, the boys learned the 10 items within 5 to 7 sessions. Trainee 3 reached the proficiency criterion in 4 additional sessions, whereas Trainee 1 required 12 more sessions. Agreement on BRS scores ranged between 90% and 93% for trainer and observer and between 87% and 95% for trainer and parents, indicating that the parents became proficient scorers of the BRS.

Mean frontalis EMG levels during the assessment periods are shown in Figure 4.6. Baseline values were generally high and variable for Trainees 1 and 2 but showed a systematic decline for Trainee 3. During BRT, EMG values declined for all children and remained at low levels at follow-up. As in the previous study, EMG levels generally paralleled the BRS scores, decreasing as relaxed behavior increased. Correlations between these two measures were $-.72$ $(p < .001)$ for Trainee 1 and $-.61$ $(p < .01)$ for Trainee 3. The correlation for Trainee 2 was not significant because of the unaccountably high EMG values in the 15th and 17th sessions.

Mean parent ratings on the Hyperactivity Index of the Conners Questionnaire are shown in Table 4.1. Each child evidenced an improvement (decrease in score) in the follow-up as compared to the baseline period. However, the changes during the BRT period differed. The scores for Trainee 1 actually increased slightly during BRT, indicating worsening behavior, but at follow-up his scores declined to within the "normal" range. Trainee 2 showed no change during training and a small improvement by the follow-up period, remaining in the "hyperactive" range. Trainee 3 had ratings in the "normal" range during baseline and showed an improvement during BRT that was maintained at follow-up.

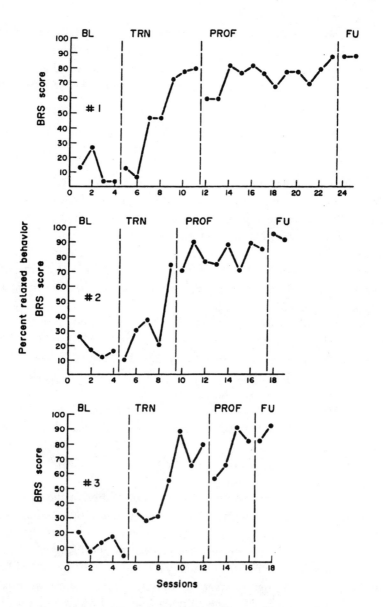

Figure 4.5: Behavioral Relaxation Scale (BRS, relaxed) Scores for Three Boys With Hyperactivity Disorder Trained by Their Parents

SOURCE: Reprinted from *Journal of Behavior Therapy and Experimental Psychiatry, 20,* V. K. Donney and R. Poppen, "Teaching Parents to Conduct Behavioral Relaxation Training With Their Hyperactive Children," 1989, pp. 319-325, with kind permission from Elsevier Science Ltd., The Boulevard, Langford Lane, Kidlington 0X5 1GB, United Kingdom.
NOTE: BL = baseline; TRN = acquisition training; PROF = proficiency training; FU = follow-up.

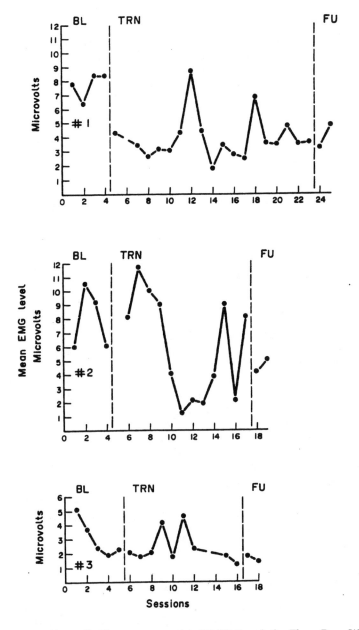

Figure 4.6: Frontalis Electromyographic (EMG) Levels for Three Boys With Hyperactivity Disorder Trained by Their Parents
SOURCE: Donney (1986).
NOTE: Phases are as designated in Figure 4.5.

Table 4.1:   Parent Ratings on the Hyperactivity Index and Home Situations Questionnaire, and Teacher Ratings on the School Situations Questionnaire, During Three Phases of Treatment

Participant	Phase	Hyperactivity Index	Home Situations Questionnaire		School Situations Questionnaire	
			Frequency (percentage)	Rating	Frequency (percentage)	Rating
1	Baseline	1.75	100	5.2	63	3.0
	Training	2.03	—	—	—	—
	Follow-up	1.15	50	3.6	75	2.0
2	Baseline	2.08	62	6.5	75	6.0
	Training	2.09	—	—	—	—
	Follow-up	1.90	40	3.7	100	7.0
3	Baseline	1.14	100	3.7	66	5.0
	Training	1.01	—	—	—	—
	Follow-up	1.00	50	2.0	51	2.5

SOURCE: Adapted from Donney (1986).

Table 4.1 also presents the scores on the Home Situations Questionnaire. For each child, the parents reported a marked improvement by follow-up, both in the percentage of situations reported as presenting a problem and in the severity rating of those situations. The School Situations Questionnaire was a different story. It should be pointed out that the teachers doing the posttraining ratings were different from the ones doing the initial rating because the children had gone to a higher grade, and so there are many confounding variables in these ratings. Trainee 1 was rated as increasing in percentage of problem situations, although the severity rating decreased. Trainee 3 was rated as improving in both percentage of situations and severity. Trainee 2 was rated as increasing in both percentage and severity. This child's teacher, on learning of his diagnosis, tried to have him moved to a special classroom, even though classroom observations indicated that the percentage of intervals he was observed to be "talking out" decreased from 23% to 8%, "out of seat" decreased from 20% to 1%, and "on-task" increased from 23% to 86%.

Discussion

This study demonstrated that parents quickly and easily learned to conduct BRT with their hyperactive children, essentially conducting training on their own after the third session. The objective criteria for relaxed behavior allowed the parents to easily observe their children and reinforce their children's performance. The parents reported that they did not maintain a formal training program; however, the children maintained the relaxed behaviors at least 2 months after training, and the parents gave anecdotal reports that they spontaneously engaged in relaxation.

Some comparisons between this and the previous study are in order. First, there were no differences in the number of sessions required to reach a proficiency criterion on the BRS. It was thought that using a beanbag chair from the outset would speed up acquisition. Perhaps this advantage was offset by the fact that parents were conducting training, but it is more likely that reaching the criterion was delayed by interruptions that occurred in the training regime as the children took time off to visit their grandmother or a divorced parent or to recover from an illness or injury. Second, it was felt that conducting training in the home would facilitate general improvement in comportment, as measured by ratings on the Conners Questionnaire. Improvements on the Hyperactivity Index during training occurred only for Trainee 3, who was not very disruptive from the start. Improvements were noted for the other two trainees, but only at follow-up. The lack of improvement during the training phase may reflect the fact that the children were home all day every day; improved parental ratings occurred only at follow-up after the children were back in school. A third point is that none of the parents maintained training after the formal program was over, although all felt that it had done much good for their children. This points up the importance of training for maintenance, perhaps through a fading and follow-up program.

SCHIZOPHRENIA

Current views of schizophrenia regard it as a disease characterized by cognitive, psychophysiological, and interpersonal deficits that result in a marked vulnerability to stress (Liberman & Corrigan, 1993). A number of studies indicate that relapse is more likely during periods of stressful life events and that persons experiencing acute episodes are characterized by high levels of arousal (Dawson, Nuechterlein, Schell, Gitlin, & Ventura, 1994; Liberman & Corrigan, 1993). Accordingly, various relaxation training methods have been tried with persons diagnosed as schizophrenic including progressive relaxation, EMG biofeedback, and meditation (e.g., Acosta, Yamamoto, & Wilcox, 1978; Pharr & Coursey, 1989; Rickard, Collier, McCoy, Crist, & Weinberger, 1993). Reduced EMG levels and improvements on self-report and clinical rating measures have been reported. Although promising, the results to date are not especially impressive, and there is little to recommend one method over another. For the reasons of simplicity and ease of training described previously, we have begun to explore the use of BRT with this population.

Teaching BRT to Persons With Schizophrenia

Noe (1997) investigated the effects of BRT with chronic schizophrenic men in an independent community living program. The men were recommended by their treatment coordinators as having high levels of anxiety, and each man volunteered to participate when the program was explained to him.

Participants

Nine men, ranging in age from 23 to 54 years and meeting *Diagnostic and Statistical Manual* criteria for chronic schizophrenia, were part of a university-affiliated independent living skills program in a large urban area. Most had histories of other problems including substance abuse, obsessive-compulsive disorder, extrapyramidal symptoms, tardive dyskinesia, mental retardation, and/or criminal activity. All were taking psychotropic medications.

Procedure

A multiple-probe-across-participants design, as described previously, was employed with three cohorts of three men in each.

During baseline, participants were asked to relax in a reclining chair in their usual fashion for about 15 minutes. Acquisition training was conducted daily to a criterion of a BRS score of at least 80% relaxed for two successive sessions with a minimum of four sessions. On reaching the criterion, the men were placed in a maintenance phase in which they had weekly assessment sessions; if they fell below 80% relaxed during maintenance, they received immediate "booster" training. Follow-up assessments were conducted 2, 4, and 6 weeks after the conclusion of maintenance. All sessions were videotaped.

Participants were instructed to practice BRT at home at least 10 minutes daily; each was given a large sign with the word "RELAX" to post in his apartment and a home practice sheet to fill out and return to the investigator. In addition, the men received various reinforcing consequences for participating. For completing a session, each man received a soda and candy bar; for completing acquisition, he received a cassette tape or tape player; for two consecutive maintenance and follow-up sessions at 80% or better, he received a T-shirt, hat, or sweatpants of his choice; and at the completion of the study, each man received $10 and dinner at a restaurant with the researcher.

The BRS was scored for a 5-minute period at the conclusion of each session. Bilateral trapezius EMG and electrodermal (EDR) activity in the right hand was measured concurrently. (The trapezius was chosen based on pilot research that indicated this site to be the most active.) The State Anxiety Inventory (Spielberger, 1983), a written self-report instrument, and the Brief Psychiatric Rating Scale (BPRS) (Lukoff, Liberman, Nuechterlein, & Ventura, 1986), a structured clinical interview, were completed at 2-week intervals. Reliability of BRS scoring was determined by a trained independent observer, blind to the study phase, who scored 25% of the videotaped observation periods; agreement ranged from 80% to 96% and averaged 87%. Reliability of BPRS scoring was determined in a similar fashion; agreement ranged from 75% to 92% and averaged 85%.

Results

The findings were fairly similar across individuals. Their data are aggregated in Table 4.2, which shows the means and ranges of scores on the dependent measures in baseline, acquisition, maintenence, and follow-up phases. Five participants reached the BRS acquisition

Table 4.2:   Mean Scores (and ranges) on Dependent Measures for Schizophrenic Participants During Phases of Treatment ($N = 9$)

Measure	Treatment Phase			
	Baseline	Acquisition	Maintenance	Follow-up
Number of sessions	7.6	4.9	5.2	3.0
	(4-12)	(4-7)	(4-8)	—
Behavioral Relaxation Scale	25.9	77.9	79.7	82.0
percentage relaxed	(11-41)	(66-92)	(65-89)	(75-92)
Electromyographic microvolts	1.1	1.2	1.3	1.1
	(0.4-2.9)	(0.5-3.5)	(0.4-3.1)	(0.5-1.7)
Electrodermal micromhos	4.7	4.7	4.5	6.4
	(1.9-7.4)	(0.5-9.4)	(1.9-7.4)	(2.7-9.3)
State Anxiety Inventory	43.6	35.1	35.8	34.4
	(27-54)	(20-49)	(23-53)	(23-51)
Brief Psychiatric Rating Scale	44.4	38.4	35.7	33.5
	(30-74)	(31-48)	(28-46)	(28-42)

NOTE: Ranges are in parentheses.

criterion of 80% or better in the minimum four sessions, and no one required more than seven. BRS scores were maintained at 80% or better for eight of nine men. EMG levels were fairly low during baseline and did not change during training. Similarly, EDR levels were generally low and consistent from baseline to training phases. Anxiety scores decreased from baseline levels for all participants; five of nine participants scored above the mean for a psychiatric population during baseline, whereas only one person did so by follow-up. BPRS scores showed similar improvements, with all participants having a decrease in ratings of their psychiatric symptoms. Five participants consistently returned their home practice sheets and four did not; there was no difference in any of the measures for those who reported practicing.

Discussion

This study demonstrated that outpatients with chronic schizophrenia could easily learn and maintain relaxed behavior and that this was associated with decreases in self-reported anxiety and other symptoms. Adjustments were made in BRT—including diaphragmatic breathing, progressive temporal requirements, and postural definitions—to meet the needs of individual clients. In contrast to other studies with this population, attrition did not occur. A major factor may have been the rich schedule of tangible and social reinforcers for participating and meeting goals. The reinforcers also may have contributed to the decrease in reported symptoms apart from any relaxation effect. Further research on this issue is needed.

Bizarre ideation sometimes intruded; for example, one man did not want to open his mouth for fear that a cockroach would crawl in. Consistent with other research (Nigl & Jackson, 1979), hallucinations and obsessive thoughts did not appear to interfere with relaxation, but they did not decrease either. BRT did not provide strong enough verbal and observational behavior alternatives to overcome these problems.

The low baseline levels on physiological measures may have created a "floor effect" that prevented improvement. Reasons for these low initial levels remain speculative.

The long-term goal of relaxation training in this population is to provide them with a means of coping with stressful events that could trigger a relapse. Preliminary data suggested some decrement in relapse rates; only one person had a "crisis" requiring intervention after BRT, but longer term follow-up is needed. To be truly effective, clients would need to be taught to use relaxation and other coping responses when they begin to become upset. Research on such a program seems warranted.

CONCLUSIONS

This chapter reviewed evidence that adults with intellectual disabilities, acquired brain injury, or schizophrenia, as well as children with hyperactivity disorder, can readily learn relaxation skills using BRT. This training has been associated with improved functioning in fine motor manipulative tasks, short-term memory tests, headache complaints, anxiety and psychiatric symptom ratings, and disruptive outbursts. More research is needed on programs to assist persons with disabilities to incorporate relaxation into their daily lives and to measure effects on activities of daily living. Promising approaches include the development of self-instructional methods, training parents or staff to conduct BRT, and group training in residential facilities. Combining BRT with other self-control methods (e.g., biofeedback, self-instructions) to provide alternatives to dysfunctional behavior in motoric, verbal, observational, and visceral modalities also should be explored.

The BRS proved useful in measuring relaxation acquisition and maintenance, particularly with persons demonstrating limited verbal capacity or anomolous physiological activity. In some instances, EMG levels were closely related to BRS scores; in others, EMG and autonomic measures were not. The reasons for the inconsistencies may be related to neurological abnormalities and medications in addition to the factors discussed in Chapter 2. On the subject of measurement, I urge researchers and clinicians to employ the BRS. The modified rating system employed by Lindsay, for example, did not allow comparisons across studies by different reseachers (Lindsay & Baty, 1986a, 1986b, 1989; Lindsay & Morrison, 1996; Lindsay et al., 1989, 1994). It would be of interest to know the level of proficiency attained by Lindsay's participants or the relationship between relaxation proficiency and attainment of target behaviors. A standardized metric, such as the BRS, facilitates communication in this field.

Finally, it was suggested that the objective nature of BRT makes it more useful than other methods for teaching relaxation to persons with disabilities. Some supportive data were reported by Lindsay (Lindsay & Baty, 1986a, 1986b, 1989; Lindsay & Morrison, 1996; Lindsay et al., 1989, 1994). But this should not be taken as a blanket prescription for BRT over other training methods. The needs and capabilities of each "special" individual should be considered in devising an intervention program, just as they are for anyone else.

5

Clinical Applications
and Extrapolations

This chapter follows up the analysis provided in Chapter 1, which described the similarities and differences of Behavioral Relaxation Training (BRT) and other relaxation training procedures. It was noted that BRT shares many features that make it effective in the treatment of disorders for which other forms of relaxation training are routinely employed. The first section of this chapter presents four case studies that illustrate the clinical use of BRT. These cases provide the practitioner with the details of treatment programs incorporating BRT and information on problems that may occur in clinical practice and their possible solutions. The second section provides a more general analysis of the classes of problems for which relaxation is prescribed, employing the same taxonomy of behavior used in the analysis of relaxation. This analysis provides a rationale for the effectiveness of relaxation and for selecting among or combining various relaxation training procedures. The third section describes considerations for combining BRT with other relaxation methods. The final section summarizes the questions that have been raised throughout the book and proposes some directions for future research and application.

CASE STUDIES OF BEHAVIORAL RELAXATION TRAINING IN CLINICAL PRACTICE

Four cases are described in which BRT was employed as the principal intervention. These cases consist of simple phobia, migraine headache, neurofacial pain, and essential tremor. They were conducted by the author or by students under his supervision.

Systematic Desensitization of a Bridge Phobia

Systematic desensitization has a long history in the treatment of phobia, representing one of the first techniques for the treatment of adult anxiety disorders to be empirically documented (Poppen, 1995; Wolpe, 1958). Helfer (1984) undertook the treatment of a phobic client, using BRT in an otherwise standard systematic desensitization framework. Special efforts were made to assess behavior in the various modalities throughout the course of treatment to determine their relationship to the outcome.

Participant

Mr. A was a 30-year-old male, married, with two children. He was a high school graduate employed in a blue-collar profession. He was referred to the university clinical center by his physician for a long-standing fear of crossing bridges.

Procedure

Social history and specific information concerning Mr. A's fears were obtained in unstructured interviews and structured fear questionnaires (Marks & Mathews, 1979; Wolpe & Lang, 1964). He also recorded instances of fearsome situations as he went about his daily affairs. Mr. A reported having a fear of crossing bridges since childhood and could recall no precipitating event. He also reported fears of his own blood and of heights. The bridge phobia interfered with his social and family life because he avoided automobile trips that necessitated crossing bridges. In instances where he had confronted bridges, he reported having his wife or friend drive while he closed his eyes during the crossing and experiencing trembling, sweating, rhinorrhea, difficulty concentrating, and embarrassment. He negotiated small highway overpasses in the course of driving to work without difficulty. Mr. A was given a rationale for systematic desensitization emphasizing the incompatibility between relaxation and anxiety.

A 19-item hierarchy was constructed involving the dimensions of people present in the car, person driving, particular bridges, time before a trip, proximity to or location on a bridge, and day or night. These were rated by Mr. A on a 100-point Subjective Unit of Disturbance Scale (Wolpe & Lazarus, 1966) and were arranged so that there was a smooth progression from low- to high-fear items. In addition, three high-intensity items (90-100 SUD) were employed as probe stimuli, inserted at various points throughout the desensitization program to determine his reaction to scenes presented out of sequence.

Dependent measures in the motoric (Behavioral Relaxation Scale [BRS], trapezius electromyographic [EMG] levels), visceral (heart rate [HR]), and verbal (self-report [Appendix A]) modalities were assessed. Observational behavior was measured informally by asking how clearly he could imagine the hierarchy items. A 5-minute observation period concluded every session, during which BRS, EMG levels, and HR were measured, followed by the verbal measure. Two baseline sessions consisted of 5 minutes of adaptation and 20 minutes of relaxing with no specific instructions. BRT sessions consisted of about 20 minutes of training. Systematic desensitization sessions consisted of 10 minutes of relaxation and about 15 minutes of item presentations. BRS, EMG levels, and HR were measured during desensitization.

Results

Relaxation training. BRT began after the start of hierarchy construction and the baseline observations. Although Mr. A's scores on the

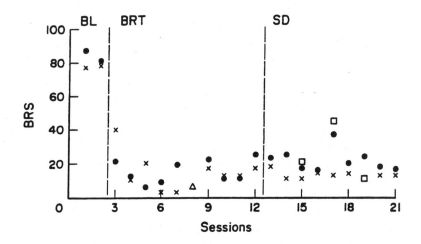

Figure 5.1: Behavioral Relaxation Scale (BRS, unrelaxed) Scores for a Man With Bridge Phobia
SOURCE: Helfer (1984).
NOTE: Phases: BL = baseline; BRT = relaxation training; SD = systematic desensitization. Legend: x's are scores during training or desensitization, dots are posttraining observations, triangles are identical scores for training and posttraining, and squares are presentations of probe items.

BRS showed rapid acquisition, as shown in Figure 5.1, his responses in other modalities indicated that a generalized response class of relaxed behaviors developed more slowly.

Specifically, Mr. A verbally reported extreme discomfort in the first BRT session, as shown in Figure 5.2. This "relaxation-induced anxiety" was related to his concern about being watched and evaluated. He felt that corrective feedback increased pressure on him to perform. Reassurance helped somewhat; a change was made to only positive feedback in the fourth BRT session, and his self-reports improved over the next six training sessions. However, without direct feedback on unrelaxed behaviors, his BRS performance worsened slightly, from 6% unrelaxed in the posttraining observation period on the third BRT session to 25% unrelaxed on the final training session (Figure 5.1). Thus, it took 10 BRT sessions before desensitization was begun.

Trapezius EMG levels, shown in Figure 5.3, were generally low and not consistently related to BRS or to self-report scores during

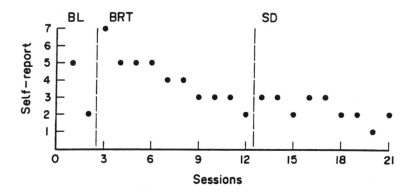

Figure 5.2: Self-Report Scores for a Man With Bridge Phobia During Posttraining Observation
SOURCE: Helfer (1984).
NOTE: Phases are as designated in Figure 5.1.

training. EMG levels increased in the first BRT session and subsequently declined, corresponding to Mr. A's self-report. But tension levels continued to vary throughout BRT.

Training-induced arousal also is indicated by increases in HR. Figure 5.4 shows that HR increased in the second BRT session but subsequently declined to rates below those in baseline. HR measures during training were slightly but consistently higher than those during the posttraining observation periods.

Systematic desensitization. After 10 minutes of relaxation with positive suggestions, Mr. A was instructed to vividly imagine a scene read by the therapist, being careful not to add other elements. He was asked to signal by raising his index finger when he had a clear image of the scene and to use the same signal if he became anxious while imagining it. Each item was presented three times for successive durations of 15, 30, and 45 seconds with approximately 30 to 60 seconds between presentations. If Mr. A exhibited additional unrelaxed behavior while imagining a scene, then the therapist provided appropriate relaxation instructions before presenting the next item. Each session began with the last scene successfully imagined in the previous session. In the middle of the third, fifth, and seventh desen-

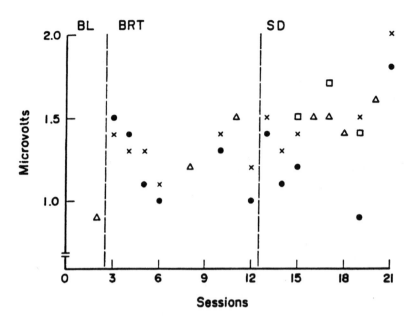

Figure 5.3: Trapezius Electromyographic Levels for a Man With Bridge Phobia
SOURCE: Helfer (1984).
NOTE: Phases and legend are as designated in Figure 5.1.

sitization sessions (Sessions 15, 17, and 19), probe items were presented for 45 seconds.

Desensitization proceeded very smoothly for Mr. A. He never signaled that he felt anxious, even to the probe items. His BRS scores were generally consistent with his (lack of) report. Figure 5.1 shows his BRS scores averaged for all scene presentations in each session. He generally displayed only one (out of nine) unrelaxed behavior— usually eyes. (Breathing was not scored due to the short time intervals.) In fact, BRS scores while imagining scenes were better than during the corresponding posttraining observation periods. BRS scores were consistent for successive presentations of the same item. Mr. A displayed increased unrelaxed behavior to the first probe item (Session 15) and a marked increase to the second probe item (Session 17); however, there was no increase during the third probe item (Session 19).

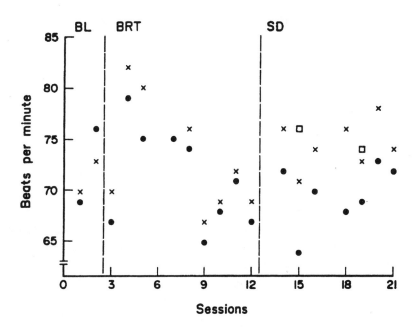

Figure 5.4: Heart Rate for a Man With Bridge Phobia
SOURCE: Helfer (1984).
NOTE: Phases and legend are as designated in Figure 5.1.

Posttraining self-report, as shown in Figure 5.2, always was in the relaxed portion of the scale (3 or less). It showed an improvement over successive desensitization sessions with a maximum level of relaxation reported after the penultimate session.

EMG levels during desensitization were slightly higher than those during BRT alone, as shown in Figure 5.3. As with BRS scores, levels during the first two probe items were elevated, but the level during the last probe showed little change. Mean EMG levels during scene presentations were equal to or slightly higher than those during posttraining observation. Figure 5.3 indicates that there was an increase in the final two desensitization sessions when the highest hierarchy items were presented. What is not shown is that EMG levels consistently declined over the successive presentations of the last two items on the hierarchy.

Figure 5.4 shows that HR, like EMG levels, was slightly higher during the desensitization sessions than during relaxation training.

Like the BRS and EMG levels, HR was elevated during the first probe item but not during the final probe. (Unfortunately, equipment failure prevented a reading during the second probe item.) HR consistently declined over successive presentations of each item and also generally declined over successive items within each session. Like EMG, HR was lower during the postsession observations than during item presentations.

In vivo assessment. After completion of the hierarchy, Mr. A accompanied the therapist on two 60-mile automobile trips to different large bridges over the Mississippi River. The therapist drove with Mr. A in the passenger seat and a technician in the rear seat to monitor HR equipment. HR was recorded at approximately 5-second intervals once the bridge was in sight. Each session consisted of two bridge crossings, over and back.

During each trip, Mr. A was alert and smiling, looking around and commenting on how easy it was. No instances of hiding his eyes, trembling, sweating, or wiping his nose were observed. HR was variable, often with high readings that may have been due to movement artifacts. Highest rates occurred at first sight of the bridge with a decline while crossing and a further decline after the crossing was complete.

Follow-up. Approximately 3 months after completion of the last in vivo assessment, Mr. A again filled out the fear questionnaires and reported on his bridge crossing activities in an interview. His fear of bridges on one questionnaire declined to a rating of 1, as did his blood/injury score. On the other fear survey, there was a slight increase in items related to blood and injury and no change with regard to heights. Mr. A reported that he had made several bridge crossings, both as driver and passenger, with no ill effects. He expressed great pleasure at his expanded social and family activities such as going to major league baseball games and big-city restaurants.

Discussion

It first appeared that BRT produced relaxation-induced anxiety, with the client reporting discomfort and manifesting elevated EMG levels and HR despite engaging in relaxed behavior as defined by the BRS. Such desynchrony points up the separability of the components of the response class called "relaxation" and the importance of multimodal assessment. This initial arousal may have contributed to the therapeutic outcome in that Mr. A learned firsthand that he could overcome anxious feelings, just as agoraphobic patients learn that their arousal is not fatal. The therapist also learned a lesson about the reactive effects of observation and the importance of adjusting the training procedure to meet the needs of individual clients, as discussed in Chapters 2 and 3.

With continued BRT, a fair degree of concurrence between response modalities was achieved. When desensitization was implemented, both concurrence and some differential responding were obvious. According to self-report (finger raising), Mr. A felt calm throughout all item presentations. But the BRS, EMG, and HR measures indicated arousal during the presentation of the first two probe items. Perhaps such arousal was not sufficient to be observed or labeled as "anxiety" by Mr. A. The effectiveness of the BRS in detecting unreported arousal may be useful to the clinician who does not have access to electronic monitoring equipment.

Overall, Mr. A learned to remain calm in motoric, verbal, and visceral modalities while imagining himself engaging in formerly fearsome behavior. How did this translate into actual practice? As discussed in a later section, one means is through a change in "rules," verbal statements about consequences for one's behavior. This was shown in Mr. A's eagerness to put his skills to the test in the in vivo assessment trips. His success on these excursions strongly reinforced his adaptive behaviors and led to continued success in his daily life.

BRT With Migraine Headache

The rationale for employing relaxation in the treatment of migraine has generally followed a stress model, focusing on visceral responses to stressful life events. Specifically, migraine sufferers are thought to respond with intercerebral vasoconstriction, followed by rebound vasodilation that produces great pain (Olton & Noonberg, 1980). Relaxation, according to this model, serves as a prophylactic, preventing or reversing the initial vasoconstrictive reaction.

Blanchard found that a program of progressive relaxation and imagery resulted in clinically significant headache reduction for approximately 26% of migraine sufferers, whereas an added program of thermal biofeedback essentially doubled the success rate (Blanchard & Andrasik, 1985). The following case was undertaken using Blanchard's protocol but substituting BRT for progressive relaxation.

Participant

Miss B was a 34-year-old unmarried woman, a college graduate employed in a managerial position with a 10-year history of headache. She referred herself for treatment to the Stress Disorders Clinic, a well-known treatment research facility. She was diagnosed by a neurologist as "classic migraine" and met the research criteria for migraine. In addition, Miss B had a diagnosis of bipolar disorder, of 6 years duration, which was controlled by lithium. She reported few current depressive symptoms; her Beck Depression Inventory score was 11 before training and was 10 at follow-up.

Procedure

Miss B received the intensive assessment battery employed by the Stress Disorders Clinic, comprised of a structured headache history interview, psychophysiological measurement, and a computerized psychological test battery (Blanchard & Andrasik, 1985).

The principal measuring instrument was the Headache Diary in which she rated her headache on a 6-point scale (0 = *no headache*, 3 = *moderate headache, pain is noticeably present*, 5 = *extremely intense headache, incapacitated*) four times daily. A weekly Headache Index was computed by summing all scores and dividing by seven, thus incorporating both frequency and intensity. She also noted all headache medications; these were scored according to a potency scale. Measures were completed for a 4-week baseline period, 4 weeks during the course of treatment, 4 weeks following treatment, and a 6-week period 6 months after completing treatment.

During each session, frontalis EMG levels, cervical trapezius EMG levels, finger temperature, and the BRS were measured in 5-minute pre- and posttraining observation periods. Self-report of relaxation was measured after each observation period.

Miss B was given a stress rationale and was told that relaxation would provide her with a means by which she could control her arousal, particularly her vascular reactions. A three-phase treatment program was outlined, each phase to consist of six sessions over a 4-week period, with 4 weeks between each phase to assess its effects before going on to the next one. The first phase was to consist of BRT, the second phase of digital temperature biofeedback, and the third phase of stress identification and problem solving. As it turned out, headache frequency was reduced to such an extent after the first phase that the other two phases were not implemented.

Reclined BRT was carried out for the first two intervention sessions. In the third and fourth sessions, diaphragmatic breathing training was added to BRT. In the fifth and sixth sessions, Upright Relaxation Training (URT), along with diaphragmatic breathing, was implemented. Homework practice of these procedures was encouraged and discussed in the treatment sessions. The use of diaphragmatic breathing and mini-relaxation throughout the day was emphasized as an immediate tool to counteract arousal and maintain calmness.

Results

Miss B learned the relaxed behaviors very rapidly. Her BRS and self-report scores were closely related (Pearson $r = .59, p < .05$). She reached 92% relaxed by the end of the second session and reported herself to be "deeply and completely relaxed." Introduction of diaphragmatic breathing resulted in an increase in unrelaxed behavior and self-report, but by the end of the next session scores again were low. Both BRS and self-report scores were elevated at the start of URT in the fifth session but decreased with training. Reclined relaxed behavior was maintained at the seventh session, an assessment session after completion of the posttraining period.

Frontalis and cervical EMG levels actually increased over the training period. These measures were quite variable and not correlated with each other or with other measures. Values in both areas were generally low at the start but decreased even more with BRT in the first two sessions. Introduction of diaphragmatic breathing resulted in tension increases in both areas. There were small increases in frontalis EMG levels and larger increases in trapezius EMG levels at the start of upright training. After URT, cervical tension showed large decreases, whereas frontalis tension increased slightly. Tension levels in both areas were higher in the posttraining assessment session than at the start of training.

Finger temperatures showed a marked increase over time. During the first session, temperature was at a moderate level, but on subsequent sessions, Miss B's pretraining temperatures started in the mid-90s, a ceiling that made further increases difficult. Temperatures were not maintained during training and often declined by about 5°. Temperatures also decreased during diaphragmatic breathing training. During URT, temperatures were high and stable. Her temperature remained high at posttraining assessment. Overall, her temperature was correlated with BRS scores (Pearson $r = .67, p < .05$).

Weekly Headache Index scores declined markedly. During baseline, Miss B experienced at least one headache per week, which she said was her usual rate. She reported one major headache the 2nd week of training and one in the 2nd week of the posttraining period but otherwise was headache free. It should be noted that this was during the holiday period, which was a generally stressful time for her. According to Blanchard's formula for calculating treatment outcome, Miss B experienced a 76% reduction in headache, well above the 50% reduction considered a "success" (Blanchard & Andrasik, 1985, p. 58). Her medication index mirrored her Headache Diary scores: baseline = 4.75, treatment = 0.00, posttreatment = 1.00, follow-up = 2.00.

During the 6 weeks of the 6-month follow-up, she reported one severe headache, which she said was the first she had experienced in the intervening period. She reported a marked decrease in frequency; however, when a headache did occur, it seemed more intense. She noted that this may have been due to her not being as "used to" the pain.

At the follow-up interview, Miss B stated that she had ceased practicing the total BRT exercises after the end of training. But she reported that she was aware of her postures and breathing and frequently engaged in mini-relaxation during the day. She felt that she was more aware of when she was becoming "uptight" and could relax in those situations. She also reported that she had started jogging, and she felt that this also contributed to her remaining headache free.

Discussion

The relationship between the various measures of relaxed behavior again points up the complexity of this response class. The close correspondence between the BRS and self-report suggested that Miss B was attending to the behaviors being trained rather than to other aspects of the situation, in contrast to Mr. A. EMG levels also corresponded to BRS and self-report scores during initial training. Miss B's initial discomfort with diaphragmatic breathing was reflected in increased tension, as was the lack of bodily support while seated in an upright posture. Finger temperature, a measure of the visceral system related to the physiological mechanism of migraine, showed a marked increase after the first training session. Although there was some temperature decrease during sessions, this measure also was correlated with BRS scores.

Based on Blanchard's findings with progressive relaxation training, we were prepared to supplement BRT with thermal biofeedback and stress management training (Blanchard & Andrasik, 1985, p. 78). This was not necessary. Although not a cure for migraine, BRT deserves further study, either by itself or in combination with other procedures. The ease with which Miss B learned the relaxed behaviors, and her concomitant reports of calm feelings, provides a counterpoint to the difficulty experienced by Mr. A. Even so, things did not happen automatically for Miss B. Diaphragmatic breathing was difficult for her to master, and it remained necessary for her to leave one hand on her abdomen to monitor her performance. But she practiced diligently, as evidenced by improvements within and between sessions, and she achieved proficiency in skills that she could use in her daily activities.

BRT With Neurofacial Pain

Self-management approaches to chronic pain recognize the important relationships among pain, physiological arousal, and negative emotions. Stress can arise from the experience of pain and dealing with limitations imposed by pain. This stress can exacerbate pain, resulting in a vicious circle leading to severe disability and emotional dysfunction. Thus, relaxation training, in its many forms, is employed as a component of many pain management programs to reduce arousal. Hanson and Gerber (1990) described incorporating the relaxed postures of BRT into their comprehensive self-management program. Lou Girodano employed BRT in a clinical case of neurofacial pain (personal communication, July 1997).

Participant

Mrs. C was a 47-year-old married woman with two children and a graduate degree in education. She was very socially active in community and church affairs, and her husband was a locally prominent figure. Six months earlier, she had been diagnosed with atypical neurofacial pain in the maxillary region of the trigeminal nerve. This had followed 3 months of medical treatment for a sinus infection. A maxillary nerve block provided complete short-term pain relief, and nerve ablation surgery was offered as a treatment option. Some have suggested that nerve-block procedures can distinguish "organic" pain from "psychological" pain, and these are used as a prelude to neural ablation surgery (Morse, 1983). However, her referring physician suggested that she try biofeedback before more invasive procedures. She took large doses of Nortriptoline and Motrin daily but reported no relief.

Procedure

Assessment was conducted using a structured interview for chronic/recurrent pain (copy available on request) and a muscle scan (Cram & Steger, 1983) of facial and neck muscles. Mrs. C monitored pain four times daily using a modification of the Headache Diary described previously. She reported almost continuous pain on the right side of her face, described as burning and throbbing, sometimes accompanied by blurred vision, varying from "moderate" to "incapacitating." The muscle scan revealed asymmetrically high readings in the right masseter, sternocleidomastoid, and cervical trapezius. Mrs. C reported clenching her jaw when upset. She reported that depression, irritability, and dread accompanied severe pain episodes and that pain interfered with her family and volunteer duties. She reported that pain was exacerbated by worry, tension, and anger and felt that there was a strong relationship between stress and pain. Life stressors, in addition to pain, included her husband's health and professional problems, severe illness of family members, demands of her volunteer commitments, and the job of raising two active sons.

Sessions were 50 minutes in duration, conducted at weekly intervals. Approximately 15 minutes was devoted to training with the balance reserved for discussion of how to implement relaxation in her daily life. After a baseline session in which she relaxed in her usual way, BRT in the reclined position was conducted for two sessions. URT occurred in the next three sessions. Each session concluded with a 5-minute observation period for BRS scoring and monitoring masseter EMG activity. She was instructed to practice relaxation at home twice daily for at least 10 minutes. In the final two sessions, a five-step mini-relaxation program was devised: stop and sit, close eyes, deep inhale, drop jaw, and exhale. These comprised a set of self-instructions that she employed throughout her heavily scheduled day. She agreed to use transitions between activities as a cue to engage in mini-relaxation. A follow-up session employing URT was conducted 2 months after training.

Results

Mrs. C's baseline BRS was a surprising 86% relaxed. With BRT, she attained BRS scores of about 97%. BRS after her first upright session dropped to 92% but subsequently increased to 100% relaxed for the remainder of training and follow-up. Masseter EMG activity was fairly high during baseline but decreased by 50% during reclined BRT and by another 50% during URT. EMG levels increased slightly during mini-relaxation practice but returned to very low levels at follow-up.

Mrs. C's daily pain ratings averaged around 3 (moderate) during baseline and did not change appreciably during reclined BRT. Her pain ratings declined to as low as 1 with URT and mini-relaxation, but she experienced increased pain during two periods in which her sister and mother-in-law were seriously ill and there were several weeks with no training. She found the mini-relaxation breaks much to her liking and reported using them 10 to 15 times daily. By follow-up, her pain ratings were about one tenth of baseline levels, and she reported large decreases in use of pain medication.

Discussion

Mrs. C presented a picture of a "hard-driving" person very concerned with fulfilling her responsibilities to family and community but angry and frightened at the limitations imposed by her pain. It was hard for her to take time for herself unless absolutely forced to stop by pain. Although she was generally aware of the relationship between stress and pain, self-monitoring and discussions with the therapist helped her to see specific instances. She reported increased awareness of tension building up and using her relaxation skills to break the stress-pain cycle. It seemed as though she might be appropriate for cognitive therapy or assertiveness training, challenging the "musts" and "shoulds" that she placed on herself. But Mrs. C recognized these situations and took steps to alter them without special intervention. A less resourceful person probably would have needed training in more coping skills than relaxation.

BRT With Essential Tremor

Essential tremor (ET) is a prevalent movement disorder that can have its onset both early and late in life (Lou & Jankovic, 1991). Three topographies of tremor are identified: resting (when the body part is fully supported), kinetic (when activity occurs), and postural (when an unsupported posture is maintained) (Findley & Capideo, 1984). ET results in significant social and functional disabilities and can be exacerbated by stress and fatigue (Busenbark, J. Nash, S. Nash, Hupple, & Koller, 1981; Jankovic, Kurland, & Young, 1989). Medication is ineffective for a sizable proportion of patients, and often there are significant side effects (Koller, 1987). Although relaxation or EMG biofeedback would appear to be useful for ET, there are a paucity of reports in the literature. Chung undertook treatment of persons with tremor disorder, one with ET and one with Parkinson's disease (Chung, 1990; Chung, Poppen, & Lundervold, 1995). His first case is described here.

Participant

Mr. D was an 86-year-old widower diagnosed with ET by a neurologist. He reported onset at age 16 years. He manifested postural
and kinetic tremor and reported disruption of activities of daily
living such as eating, drinking, and dressing. He no longer wrote
because of arthritis but reported that tremor had affected his writing.
He lived alone and participated in community senior citizen activities. He took 230 milligrams of Mysoline daily throughout the study.

Procedure

A multiphase design was employed consisting of baseline (four
sessions), BRT (reclined, eight sessions), URT (four sessions), and
follow-up (one session). Sessions were conducted once or twice
weekly. In baseline, Mr. D relaxed in his usual fashion for 10 minutes
both while seated in an upright postion and while reclined. During
BRT, training was conducted for 15 to 20 minutes. In four sessions
during this phase, Mr. D also was asked to relax in the upright chair
to determine whether there was any transfer from reclined to upright
relaxation. After reaching a criterion of at least 85% relaxed in the
reclined position for three consecutive sessions, Mr. D was trained in
upright relaxation to the same criterion. Follow-up was conducted 2
weeks after the last training session. He was instructed to practice
relaxation at home every day for at least 15 minutes.

The BRS was scored during a 5-minute observation period at the
conclusion of baseline and BRT sessions. Postural tremor for both
right and left hands was assessed at the end of each observation
period by asking Mr. D, while seated, to extend his arm slowly in
front, with wrist extended and hand open, and to maintain this
position for 20 seconds. Kinetic tremor was assessed by asking him
to extend his right and left arms as before, to touch his nose with
extended forefinger, and to return to rest. EMG levels of the forearm
flexors and extensors during these maneuvers were recorded, and
tremor was rated using the Clinical Rating of Tremor Scale (CRTS)
(Fahn, Toloso, & Marin, 1988). Mr. D rated his own tremor within
each session and was given a self-rating sheet for tremor severity at
home that targeted activities of eating, drinking, and dressing.

Results

Mr. D rapidly learned most of the relaxed postures, achieving 80% during the first BRT session. He required several more sessions to reach the 85% criterion and achieved nearly 100% in the last session. There was no transfer from reclined to upright relaxation; he remained at around 50% relaxed until URT was given, at which time he rapidly reached the criterion. BRS scores were about 80% relaxed for both reclined and upright at follow-up.

Forearm EMG values during postural and kinetic tremor tests decreased steadily throughout relaxation training for both right and left arms. EMG levels were slightly but consistently higher in the right arm than in the left arm, and levels were higher in kinetic testing than in postural testing. By follow-up, EMG values for both arms were one third their baseline levels for the postural test and one half their baseline levels for the kinetic test.

CRTS scores for both postural and kinetic tremor also showed marked improvement after BRT. Baseline scores were in the "mild" to "moderate" range and decreased to the "mild" to "no tremor" range with several zero scores in BRT, URT, and follow-up sessions. Mr. D's self-ratings within sessions, as well as his daily "global" and eating ratings, also improved to "very mild" and zero levels. The therapist took Mr. D out to eat after the follow-up and informally observed no tremor.

Discussion

This case supported the use of forearm EMG levels, in which agonist-antagonist muscle groups were monitored, as a means of assessing tremor. Accelerometry has been used in basic research on tremor (Elble & Koller, 1990), but this equipment is complex and much less accessible to the clinician than is EMG equipment. Tremor ratings are routinely employed in clinical work, but there is little research on their reliability and validity. Efforts toward providing interventions for tremor disorders also must be directed at the issue of assessment (Lundervold & Poppen, 1995).

This case demonstrated that age is no barrier to learning BRT and that disorders having a neurological basis can be ameliorated by relaxation. Chung also found positive benefits of BRT on dysfunctions related to Parkinson's disease (Chung et al., 1995). The effectiveness of BRT with ET has been replicated in several more cases (Lundervold, 1995), and this approach has been extended to ataxia in persons with acquired brain injury (Guercio, Chittum, & McMorrow, 1997; Guercio, Ferguson, & McMorrow, in press; see Chapter 4). Although primarily thought of as a motoric disorder, tremor has many emotional and social sequelae that may require intervention in additional response modalities (Lundervold & Poppen, 1995). Nevertheless, BRT provides a promising intervention with a class of disorders for which there are few treatment alternatives.

TARGETS OF RELAXATION TRAINING

Wolpe's (1958) seminal book, *Psychotherapy by Reciprocal Inhibition*, sparked the widespread interest in relaxation training for anxiety and stress disorders (Poppen, 1995). Wolpe proposed that the visceral responses resulting from progressive relaxation training were incompatible with and "reciprocally inhibited" the visceral responses characteristic of anxiety. The present book also proposes an incompatibility hypothesis, but across a wider spectrum of behaviors. As presented in Chapter 1, relaxation is viewed not as a unidimensional internal state but rather as a response class across four modalities that may differ among individuals and situations. Just as relaxation is a complex behavior, the behaviors for which relaxation is employed as an antidote also are multidimensional. This book proposes that relaxed behaviors provide adaptive alternatives to complex emotional, stress, and pain behavior response classes.

A Taxonomy of Problematic Behavior

Table 5.1 presents a taxonomy of problematic behavior analogous to the earlier presentation of relaxation behaviors. Only an outline is provided with frequently occurring behavior given as examples. For each response class, not all behaviors occur in all individuals in all situations, but there is enough consistency to give rise to a class name such as "phobia" or "back pain." BRT provides alternatives to problematic behavior in each modality. Other relaxation methods that

Table 5.1:   Taxonomy of Problematic Behavior: Disorders for
Which Relaxed Behavior Provides an Alternative

Disorder	*Behavior Modality*			
	Motoric	*Verbal*	*Visceral*	*Observational*
Anxiety	Avoidance, muscle tension	Rules, complaints	Increased heart rate, hyperventilation	Phobic imagery, vigilance, attend to fear
Anger	Aggression, muscle tension	Rules, threats, curses	Increased heart rate, increased blood pressure	Perceive insult, attend to rage
Chronic pain	Guarding, bracing, muscle spasm, inactivity	Rules, grimace, complaints, requests for help	Hyperventilation, sighs, crying	Attend to pain, seek distraction
Migraine headache	Muscle tension, avoidance	Rules, complaints	Nausea, vasoactivity	Aura, photophobia, attend to pain
Type A behavior	Hurried activity, muscle tension	Rules about time and competition, forced speech	Increased heart rate, increased blood pressure	Attend to time cues, performance standards
Asthma	Avoidance	Rules, complaints	Wheeze, gasp	Vigilance, attend to breathing

emphasize particular modalities may provide additional help for particular disorders or individual clients. This schema provides a basis for selecting among the various training methods; a relaxation procedure that targets behavior in a particular modality is expected to be especially effective in overcoming maladaptive behavior in that modality. Illustrations of this analysis are given for emotional, pain, and stress response classes.

Emotional Problem: Anxiety

Anxiety has been the dominant focus of behavior therapy since its inception and has been the primary target of relaxation theories and therapies. Classification of anxiety problems is based on antecedent events that are believed to trigger the anxiety response. Thus, phobias are related to specific social and physical environmental events (e.g., agoraphobia to internal and external events), and generalized anxiety is defined by the absence of particular antecedents. A complete account of anxiety problems and their treatments is beyond the scope of this book, but an analysis of anxiety according to the taxonomy given in Table 5.1 describes the uses of relaxation as an adaptive alternative in each response modality.

The goal of BRT is to counter anxious behavior in the four modalities. Although training usually is carried out in a quiet environment, transferring skills to the "real-life" environment is an important therapeutic goal. Methods of transfer include "train and hope," simple exposure, and graded exposure with imaginal, pictorial, or in vivo cues. As with other relaxation training procedures, BRT is assumed to have prophylactic effects in which regular practice in the home and work environments makes the trainee less susceptible to anxious arousal to evoking stimuli. An important factor governing this effect, as well as effectiveness in combating anxiety once aroused, is the ease with which relaxed behaviors can be emitted in the natural environment.

Motoric Anxious Behavior

As shown in Table 5.1, this modality commonly includes avoidance of certain situations and events. When confronted with a fearsome situation or even a few cues associated with such an event, motoric behavior such as increased muscle tension, "freezing" or restlessness, and (if possible) escape is likely. Thus, a person who fears flying will avoid that mode of travel, and a person with public speaking anxiety will avoid professional commitments requiring such performance. Mr. A avoided travel that required crossing bridges. When avoidance is not possible, increased muscle tension of the hands, arms, legs, and shoulders leads to "white knuckles," trembling, and/or pacing. A person with generalized anxiety, not associated with any particular event, is likely to display frequent restlessness and aimless activity.

Relaxed motoric behavior is the primary emphasis of BRT. It is incompatible with actively avoiding or escaping a situation, and it counters the tension and restlessness that characterize anxious arousal. Placing himself or herself in relaxed postures is an overt action that a person can take when confronted with an aversive situation. This provides an experiential basis for a person to observe himself or herself as calm and in control. Mr. A displayed relaxed motoric behavior while imagining the aversive scenes during desensitization.

Verbal Anxious Behavior

This mode of anxiety includes reports of environmental events and of the individual's reactions to them. In clinical or research settings, these statements are solicited on standardized lists and scales. Anxious verbal behavior may be formulated in terms of "rules" (Poppen, 1989) that exaggerate the aversiveness of the antecedent situation (e.g., spiders are especially huge and hairy, airplanes are incredibly noisy and unstable), emphasize the magnitude of the response (e.g., "My heart is pounding so fast it will burst," "I can't breathe"), and magnify the consequences of arousal (e.g., "I'm going to die!" "I can't stand this!"). A frequent rule concerns the anxious person's lack of control and inability to cope. Mr. A stated that he could not control his reactions when faced by a bridge and, thus, was incapable of driving. "Worry" can be regarded as excessive verbal rehearsal of negative antecedents, behaviors, or consequences. Such frequent or extreme verbal statements can add to the cycle of arousal, producing additional tension, visceral upset, and narrowed observation.

Verbal behavior is controlled not only by the events being described but also by audience variables such as attention and aid. External audience control is likely to be weak in that anxious persons will address their comments to people to whom they would not ordinarily speak such as the hapless stranger in the airplane seat next to a phobic flyer. Also, a person can serve as his or her own audience; a worrier "listens" to his or her own negative accounts with increasing upset.

Relaxed verbal behavior is generated by the BRT list of 10 "labels" of relaxed items, which the person can covertly recite during practice. Self-statements on how to relax and be calm also provide a reminder to the individual that he or she has a coping skill to employ in upsetting situations. Such statements are incompatible with anxious rules and may aid relaxation in other modalities as well. For example, verbal review of the relaxed behaviors can serve as cues to reduce tension and calm breathing and can also focus observation on adaptive rather than maladaptive responding. It is unlikely that verbal relaxation alone is sufficient to counteract anxious rules, and additional interventions to replace this response category are needed. Mr. A's verbal description of his behavior and its consequences showed a marked change after desensitization with BRT, and he confidently looked forward to the in vivo assessment.

Visceral Anxious Behavior

This domain of anxious behavior is characterized by heightened "fight-or-flight" autonomic activity, although wide individual differences exist and objective measurement often is difficult. Commonly noticed reactions include rapid and pounding pulse, pallor, and cold extremities in the cardiovascular system; rapid, shallow breathing and dizziness in the respiratory system; sweaty palms, armpits, and upper lip in the sudomotor system; and "butterflies," nausea, dry mouth, and stomach rumbling in the digestive system. Mr. A reported the unusual response of a runny nose. In some cases, such activity is more severe prior to the actual event, as in "stage fright" or "performance anxiety." Anxious visceral behavior may diminish as soon as the situation is over, or it may persist for some time afterward. Some individuals respond viscerally to stimuli associated with the fearsome situation such as a verbal description or a pictorial presentation, whereas others discriminate these events from the "real thing" and do not react to symbols. In cases of panic, the individual reacts to sensations of visceral arousal with increased anxiety.

BRT teaches breathing control, directly counteracting the rapid shallow breathing that often is part of some anxiety response classes including panic. Other visceral systems may be influenced by slow, regular breathing and by decreases in muscle activity through relaxed postures. However, which systems are affected in what individuals under what circumstances remain a matter for further research. The absence or reduction of anxious visceral responding can serve as the basis for the observation and reporting of feelings of calmness and control. Mr. A experienced cardiac acceleration on initial sighting of a bridge during in vivo assessment, but he did not observe this as aversive.

Observational Anxious Behavior

This anxious response mode is characterized by close attention to one's own visceral activity and muscle tension and vigilance for external environment cues that might signal the onset of an aversive situation. In line with this narrowed attending, the magnitude of fearsome events and reactions often is exaggerated, verifying the anxious rules described previously. The person scans his or her environment for signs of impending doom and often misinterprets events in accordance with this view. Any creak or lurch of an aircraft is indicative of a crash, any insect is seen as a poisonous spider, or any evaluation is seen as criticism. Similarly, one's own behavior also is magnified by close observation. One is "drenched" with sweat, one's heart "almost bursts" from pounding, or one "almost dies" from breathlessness. A person may close his or her eyes and ears to avoid or escape external stimulation, but covert events are more difficult to ignore.

As already described, relaxed postures and breathing provide a focus for relaxed observational behavior. This is both diversionary, distracting the person from attending to aversive external and internal events, and constructive, allowing the perception of control. Without the overwhelming perception of external threats and internal collapse, a person is better able to observe the relevant features of the environment for adaptive problem solving. During desensitization, Mr. A covertly observed the scenes on the hierarchy as well as his own calm behavior.

Conclusions: Anxiety

Relaxed behaviors provide effective alternatives for many members of the anxiety response class, but there are many other aspects of anxiety that are not addressed by relaxation training alone. Relaxing in the face of aversive or threatening cues may facilitate more effective coping responses. A total behavioral program for anxiety problems requires a rationale for undergoing training, systematic exposure to fearsome situations, training in active and adaptive coping skills, a reformulation of rules, social reinforcement for improvements, and constructive support for setbacks.

Chronic Pain Problems

Thanks to the pioneering work of Fordyce (1976), it is widely recognized that chronic pain is not a simple neurological response to tissue damage but rather is a complex class of behavior strongly influenced by social contingencies. Many aspects of pain behavior can be described by the taxonomy given previously and lend themselves to treatment by BRT.

Unlike acute or episodic pain, chronic pain always is present, although it may wax and wane in intensity. This makes initial training difficult because it requires the trainee to immediately change some pain behaviors on starting treatment such as inactivity and attending to pain. On the other hand, this decreases the problem of transfer because the problem is less specific to particular environments.

Motoric Pain Behavior

As illustrated in Table 5.1, chronic lower back pain is characterized by many problems in the motoric domain. Guarding and bracing refer to stiff and awkward postures and movements to protect the back (Keefe & Block, 1982). Such action results in heightened muscle tension and asymmetric activity in many parts of the body in addition to the tension and asymmetry in the lower back. Inactivity refers to long periods of sitting or laying down, leading to muscle atrophy. Generalized muscle tension and inactivity are characteristic of most types of pain regardless of the site or physiological mechanism. Mrs. C evidenced increased tension in face and neck muscles.

Inasmuch as BRT does not require muscular contraction, it is likely to be especially effective with conditions involving muscles that are already tense or in spasm. Similar considerations are important for joint problems such as arthritis. BRT's emphasis on symmetry of postures also is beneficial for the twisted products of guarding and bracing, although it is difficult to achieve in early stages of training. A gradual approach is recommended. Supplementary training of particularly troublesome muscle groups with EMG biofeedback, as discussed later in this chapter, provides a useful adjunct to BRT. EMG monitoring of affected muscle groups is a useful adjunct to relaxation training. Mrs. C's masseter muscle activity decreased, making bio-feedback unnecessary.

Verbal Pain Behavior

This modality includes reporting discomfort to others, primarily for the consequences of attention and aid. Such aid has little lasting effect; over a period of time, the sympathy of friends, family, and medical staff may extinguish, resulting in escalating intensity and frequency of complaints and demands. Negative rules about pain are formulated concerning antecedents (e.g., incompetence of doctors, greed of lawyers, indifference of family), behavior (e.g., incapacity to function, magnitude of pain), and consequences (e.g., nothing will change, insurance will run out). A pain sufferer often expresses angry statements of the failure of others to provide relief and depressive statements of helplessness and hopelessness. Such rules may increase pain by creating an aversive social environment and focusing the sufferer's attention on his or her ailments and incapacities. Mrs. C was unusual in this respect in that she was not a "complainer." Nevertheless, she provided a private audience as she worried about her pain condition, similar to the self-talk characteristic of anxiety described previously.

BRT provides some alternatives to verbal pain behavior. As in the case of anxiety, the list of relaxed labels provides a prompt for trainees to engage in relaxed activities. The self-reminder of a coping skill can serve as an alternative to statements of helplessness. It also can direct observation toward adaptive rather than unadaptive behavior and sensations. Mrs. C found the list of mini-relaxation activities to be a useful prompt to take frequent short breaks rather than letting tension build as she hurried from one task to another.

Visceral Pain Behavior

This modality has not received much attention in chronic pain. Breathing irregularities, such as rapid shallow breathing and deep sighs, are common in lower back and other pain conditions. Responses such as sweating, pallor, or nausea may occur in some people during a severe pain episode.

BRT targets visceral relaxation primarily through breathing control, which counteracts hyperventilation. As described earlier, diaphragmatic breathing and decreased muscle tension also may have salutary effects on various channels of autonomic arousal.

Observational Pain Behavior

As with anxiety, this modality is a major component of pain behavior. Close attention to pain and discomfort magnifies these sensations and can crowd out observation of any other events. Muscle tension, autonomic activity, and limitations of action serve as major foci of observation. A sufferer may seek to distract himself or herself through passive observational behavior such as watching television. Mrs. C attempted to use distraction by "keeping her mind busy" as a means of coping with pain, but without much success.

BRT promotes a focus on self-control and adaptive behaviors of relaxed postures and breathing. Because bodily cues often are overwhelmingly aversive, it may be useful to supplement BRT with a procedure that diverts attention from this dimension. Guided imagery, which emphasizes other types of sensory cues, may be particularly helpful in this respect. Mrs. C found that she became increasingly aware of low levels of tension in her face, which she could control through relaxation as opposed to ignoring pain until it increased to unmanageable levels.

Conclusions: Chronic Pain

BRT can serve as a useful component in a chronic pain treatment program but cannot be regarded as a panacea. Even within the domain of relaxation, it may be necessary to supplement BRT with additional procedures to overcome pain behavior in particular modalities. EMG biofeedback is recommended for treatment of specific muscle groups and guided imagery for control of observational behavior. In addition, systematic contingency management programs often are needed to overcome inactivity and social dependency. Medication withdrawal, vocational and leisure skill training, and family education all are important aspects of a comprehensive pain management program.

Stress Problem: Migraine Headache

Behavioral treatment of stress-related disorders has greatly increased over the past decade. Dualistic mind/body formulations are particularly prevalent (e.g., Stoyva, 1977). Stress responses are considered to have physiological and psychological components analogous to somatic and cognitive anxiety. Physiologically, stress is regarded as an imbalance, primarily in the autonomic nervous system but also involving hormonal, immune, and skeletal-muscular systems. Psychological predispositions are considered to be important mediators of physiological activity. Thus, according to this view, one's personality, response style, or mood influences one's bodily reactions to the demands of everyday life.

Physiological abnormalities define many stress disorders such as asthma, coronary heart disease, and Raynaud's disease. In other disorders, notably headache and myofacial pain-dysfunction, the physiological responses are not apparent and there is disagreement over what systems are involved.

Psychologically, scores on questionnaires concerning anxiety, depression, assertiveness, locus of control, affect, multiphasic personality, hostility, and so forth often are found to be associated with various disorders. The most extensively researched relationship is that between "Type A personality" and coronary heart disease (Booth-Kewley & Friedman, 1987). There also is a sizable literature on personality, and headache (Blanchard & Andrasik, 1985). The magnitudes of the relationships are small, but there is general consensus on an association between "negative affect" scores, such as anxiety and depression, and stress disorders. The direction of causality is not certain, and perhaps it is more fruitful to regard these relationships as interdependent; that is, anxious and depressive behaviors may well be members of the same response classes as stress disorders, all of which are in need of replacement by adaptive alternative behavior.

Rather than the dualistic approach, stress disorders can be considered to be response classes encompassing the four behavioral modalities as outlined in Table 5.1. Relaxation training, as well as other components of a treatment program, aim to modify behavior within and across these categories.

Migraine, like many stress disorders, is episodic, although it is assumed that there are characteristic interepisodic behaviors that cumulate or otherwise predispose a person to an attack. Treatments are aimed at modifying these behaviors, thereby reducing the frequency of episodes; only secondarily is treatment concerned with what to do when an attack occurs. According to this view, regular practice of relaxed behaviors restores equilibrium to an imbalanced vascular system, making the system less likely to cross some threshold into a maladaptive range. Once the throes of an attack have begun, relaxation may promote restoring balance.

Motoric Migraine Behavior

Chronic elevated muscle tension in the head and neck usually is thought of as characteristic of muscle contraction headache, but there is evidence that levels are even higher in migraine sufferers (Blanchard & Andrasik, 1985; Olton & Noonberg, 1980). Some migraine sufferers display the busy, nonstop response style termed "Type A." Overt motoric behavior during a migraine episode is notably limited, as the sufferer often ceases all activity and lies down during a severe attack. Muscle tension, especially of the head and neck, may be markedly increased, resulting in additional pain.

BRT practiced on a regular basis, especially mini-relaxation of the face and shoulders throughout the day, can reduce chronic tension. Longer practice periods can provide respite from a harried schedule but need not be so long as to add to a person's time pressure. During the onset of full-blown occurrence of a headache, relaxation can reduce the pain-induced tension cycle. Like Mrs. C, Miss B found mini-relaxation to be especially useful and practiced it regularly.

Verbal Migraine Behavior

Between headache episodes, verbal behavior may be characterized by the "rules" typical of anxiety, depression, nonassertion, and so forth. A focus on environmental aversiveness and behavioral incapacity can interfere with effective problem solving and increase environmental stressors. During a headache episode, verbal behavior is like that of chronic pain patients, with an emphasis on the intolerability of the situation.

As in the cases of anxiety and pain, the relaxed verbal behavior of BRT provides an alternative to the usual rules plus the reminder that the person has a coping skill. The labels can cue relaxed motoric, visceral, and observational behaviors during regular practice periods as well as during headache episodes. Miss B originally thought of her headache as the inevitable product of hormonal or other factors over which she had no control. She replaced this view with rules concerning her own ability to control her reactions. Others might find that autogenic phrases contribute additional help in controlling visceral and observational behavior.

Visceral Migraine Behavior

Visceral activity plays a leading role in most formulations of migraine (Olton & Noonberg, 1980). Between episodes, migraine sufferers supposedly are characterized by vasomotor lability, with a tendency to respond to stressful events with peripheral and intracranial vasoconstriction. They may observe these events as cold hands and feet and as visual or other sensory prodromes. The headache itself is related to intracranial vasodilation occurring as a "rebound" to prolonged constriction. Gastrointestinal distress may precede or accompany the headache.

Reduced muscle tension and diaphragmatic breathing resulting from BRT may have a preventive or restorative effect on labile vascular activity during nonheadache periods. Miss B showed increased peripheral temperature after the first BRT session, and her temperatures were correlated with BRS scores. Thermal biofeedback directly targets peripheral vascular activity and may act synergistically with BRT in promoting vascular control.

Observational Migraine Behavior

During nonheadache periods, migraine sufferers may be characterized by vigilance for events associated with headache, similar to anxious observational behavior. Some may be alert for foods causing vascular reactions. Others may be sensitized to events that are troublesome during a headache such as bright lights, odors, or nausea related to menstruation. One migraine sufferer believed that bright lights precipitated his headaches and wore dark glasses all the time. During a headache episode, sufferers try to decrease overt observation, darkening their rooms and insisting on quiet. Covert observation of pain and nausea may be particularly acute, similar to chronic pain patients.

Relaxed observational behavior in migraine sufferers functions similarly to that described for anxiety and pain. During nonheadache periods, it promotes the perception of control. Additional therapy procedures may be necessary to deal with "superstitious" associations between environmental events and headache and to promote functional observation of headache factors. During a headache, observation of relaxed postures and breathing may divert some of the focus on discomfort and promote a feeling of control. As with chronic pain, imagery procedures may enhance the redirection of observation.

Conclusions: Migraine

BRT targets many migraine behaviors but may not provide a complete program by itself, notwithstanding Miss B's success. Within the realm of relaxation, additional emphasis on verbal behavior (provided by autogenic training), on visceral behavior (provided by thermal biofeedback), and on observational behavior (provided by guided imagery) may be expected to facilitate treatment. In addition to relaxation procedures, a comprehensive migraine treatment program should include an analysis of possible dietary factors. For many individuals, training in social and interpersonal skills such as assertiveness, communication, or time management can make their environments less stressful. As with other disorders, rules emphasizing self-control and competence should be promoted.

Summary

Relaxation training is an integral part of the behavioral treatment of many disorders. The analysis presented in this section proposes that relaxation is effective not because it is a hypothetical neurological or psychological state that reciprocally inhibits another maladaptive neurological or psychological state but rather because the specific, observable relaxed behaviors provide adaptive alternatives to the numerous problematic behaviors that comprise a clinical entity. The various relaxation training methods emphasize particular response domains, which correspond in varying degrees to the problems characteristic of particular clinical categories and to the idiosyncratic needs of individual clients. This analysis provides a rational basis for developing treatment programs and generates many hypotheses awaiting empirical verification.

COMBINING BEHAVIORAL RELAXATION TRAINING WITH OTHER RELAXATION PROCEDURES

As outlined in Chapter 1, the various relaxation training methods emphasize different behavioral domains and particular responses within these domains. Although BRT encompasses all four modalities, it does not cover all possible responses within each one. In cases of particular disorders (as described in the preceding section) or to meet the needs of individual trainees, it could be helpful to broaden the scope of relaxed behaviors by incorporating several methods.

A Shotgun Approach

One strategy is to employ a "shotgun" approach combining many methods in the hope that some aspect will be appropriate for the idiosyncratic needs of each trainee. This approach has been advocated for a variety of behavior change programs (e.g., Azrin, 1977). An example specific to relaxation is the migraine headache program of Blanchard and Andrasik (1985), which combines progressive relaxation training, autogenic phrases, thermal biofeedback, and guided imagery, thus targeting motoric, verbal, visceral, and observational behavior modalities.

An advantage of a shotgun approach is that it increases the likelihood of hitting a problematic behavior when the relevant variables are not known. In a research setting, it offers the opportunity of analyzing a large database after completion of treatment and relating client variables to treatment and outcome variables. In this way, a treatment program can be refined to ultimately include only procedures pertinent to each individual. Refinement is important because the shotgun approach can result in the trainer and trainee wasting time on unnecessary or even counterproductive procedures.

Specific Combinations

In the best of worlds, a comprehensive behavior analysis of each client would reveal the specific domains requiring treatment. Specific relaxation methods to counteract particular problematic responses could then be selected. Following is a discussion of the ways in which particular combinations of BRT and other training methods could prove complementary.

Progressive Relaxation and BRT

Both methods emphasize the motoric domain, but there are several ways in which they supplement each other. First, when BRT is the primary training method, some individuals might have difficulty with a particular item. If this happens, then a tense-release exercise of the relevant musculature aids in teaching control of that area. The control gained through increasing and then decreasing tension may be seen as successive approximations toward sustaining a relaxed posture. For example, some people have difficulty with *eyes,* continuing to move their eyes beneath closed eyelids. Verbal feedback may prove frustrating because the trainees are unable to directly control this action. Squeezing the eyes tightly closed has the effect of stabilizing the eyeballs as well as directing observation to the proprioceptive sensations of tightness. Progressively releasing the tension allows the eyeballs to remain stationary while maintaining the trainees' focus on the muscular sensations.

When progressive relaxation training is the primary method, BRT is helpful in showing trainees how their bodies should appear when the tension is released and in aiding the release of tension in particular muscle groups. For example, in jaw exercises for the masseter and temporalis muscles, people release the "clench" but often leave the jaw in a closed position. By training the relaxed open posture defined as *mouth,* trainees are more likely to completely release the tension in the jaw muscles.

EMG Biofeedback and BRT

EMG biofeedback is another motoric procedure that can supplement BRT in training a specific muscle group. For example, in learning diaphragmatic breathing, some trainees have difficulty in not using their trapezius muscles. Their shoulders continue to rise and fall despite their best efforts to use only their diaphragms. EMG feedback from the trapezius provides the trainees with information of shoulder activity that ordinarily is imperceptible. Thus, observation of this external signal can aid in learning breathing control.

The supplementary use of EMG biofeedback in treating chronic back pain has been mentioned. BRT teaches symmetry and generally reduced tension throughout the body. However, certain muscle groups may be hyperactive or spasmodic and may prohibit achieving relaxed postures in particular areas. For example, high and asymmetric tension levels in the spinea erectors could be troublesome, particularly in an upright seated position. EMG biofeedback focusing on those muscles would be synergistic to the overall goals of BRT.

When EMG biofeedback is the training method of choice, BRT can provide a "platform" from which to begin training. As noted previously, EMG biofeedback often may serve as an indirect way in which to teach relaxed postures (Poppen, Hanson, & Ip, 1988; Schilling & Poppen, 1983); that is, trainees learn to reduce the feedback signal by reducing movements and shifting their postures into relaxed ones. If still lower levels can be achieved than those reached by assuming relaxed postures, then initial BRT would be an efficient first phase, to be followed by biofeedback. This has been a useful strategy in addressing tremor disorders (Guercio et al., in press; Lundervold, 1995).

Thermal Biofeedback and BRT

Thermal biofeedback targets control of behavior in the visceral modality, namely vascular control (usually vasodilation). The controversy over the source of its efficacy—whether such control is achieved directly or indirectly through mediation in other behavior domains—has been described previously. A clinical goal may simply be to achieve warm hands without regard to the mechanism, for example, in the treatment of Raynaud's disease. In the long run, of course, it is important to be able to specify the controlling variables, which may differ across individuals. Until research untangles this knot, a shotgun approach may be useful. BRT reduces general muscle tension, which may contribute to vasodilation. Diaphragmatic breathing also may produce vasodilation (Bacon & Poppen, 1985; Boyer & Poppen, 1995). Training persons in these skills provides a means by which they might be able to achieve success in hand warming. In addition, similar to the point already made with respect to EMG biofeedback, BRT can provide a foundation on which to build additional vascular control.

Autogenic Training and BRT

Autogenic training targets verbal behavior, which in turn is assumed to control responding in the other domains. As with EMG and thermal biofeedback training, BRT can provide a basis from which any additional effects of autogenic phrases may be assessed. From another point of view, BRT does not require much from the trainees in the way of verbal and observational behavior, and some individuals may "let their minds wander" to events inconsistent with relaxation. Autogenic phrases provide an adaptive alternative to arousing thoughts. The verbal and observational behavior targeted by autogenic training can supplement the labels and observation of postures provided by BRT.

Guided Imagery and BRT

Similar to autogenic training, the emphasis of this procedure on verbal and observational behavior could provide a useful supplement to BRT in cases in which attentional control is particularly difficult. For example, in chronic pain, the observational focus on imagery-constructed sensory events may provide an effective alternative to attending to pain. In combination with the motoric relaxation produced by BRT, this seems a potent package for countering many aspects of pain behavior.

DIRECTIONS FOR FUTURE RESEARCH

The basic empirical foundations for BRT and the use of the BRS have been presented. But many assertions about relaxation in general, and about BRT and the BRS in particular, are hypotheses requiring verification. This final section brings together a number of questions raised throughout the book. These issues fall under two general headings, one dealing with the basic nature of relaxation and the other encompassing its clinical significance. This is admittedly a somewhat fuzzy distinction in that relaxation always is employed for clinical goals. However, some questions pertain to relaxation regardless of the particular clinical outcome, whereas others are more directly concerned with clinical results.

Basic Research Questions

The fundamental issue remains the same: What is the nature of relaxation? Like Kipling's blind men and the elephant, various investigators have asserted that relaxation is, among other things, parasympathetic dominance, motoneuron quiescence, or a cognitive state of calm. Ignoring the problems of assessment for the moment, each of these may be part of the picture but none is the whole "elephant." Perhaps a better metaphor would be the chameleon, reflecting the idea that relaxation is different things in different situations for different people. As presented in this book, relaxation is a response class across four behavior domains; the elements of this class differ depending on environmental and individual variables. This point of view might be seen as enormously complicating the matter, greatly expanding the number of variables that must be considered. On the other hand, by changing the focus from a search for an elusive "state" to a functional analysis of behavior, the chameleon can be better described.

What Are Common and Specific Effects?

A major question concerns what often are termed "placebo" effects. These may be more accurately called the effects of the "common elements" of relaxation training procedures, as discussed in Chapter

1. The distinction is that common elements are not inert procedures (as implied by the term "placebo") but rather are active variables influencing behavior. Because they are an inextricable part of most training procedures, it is difficult to control for them by omission; that is, the appropriate research design is not a comparison of the presence versus the absence of these variables (as in "double-blind" medical research) but rather is a comparison of qualities and levels of these elements.

Common treatment elements involve certain antecedents, behaviors, and consequences. The antecedents typically include "rules" or the rationale for training, an authority with special knowledge, an unwanted condition for which relaxation is said to be helpful, and a quiet place for training and practice. The behaviors include routine cessation of ongoing activities, observation of a repetitive low-intensity event, a comfortable posture, and self-report of progress. The consequences include social approval for success, social support for failure, and possible alleviation of the unwanted condition.

The issue of interest is as follows: What does BRT (or any relaxation procedure) add to this general format? What are the effects of engaging in particular relaxed postures and observing oneself doing so, as opposed to engaging in some other motoric and observational behavior? More generally, as outlined in Table 1.2, what are the effects of engaging in any of the behaviors recommended by particular training methods based on various theories of relaxation? Research comparing various relaxation methods is beginning to address these questions, but this cannot be done in blanket terms of "better" or "worse." Effects in all behavior modalities must be considered. Efforts to detect changes within and across modalities other than the targeted ones should be increased. For example, within the motoric domain, we have found that EMG biofeedback for reducing tension produces relaxed postures (Poppen et al., 1988) and that producing relaxed postures reduces EMG levels (Poppen & Maurer, 1982). But what are the effects of motoric training on verbal, visceral, and observational behaviors? Similarly, verbally guided observational procedures, such as autogenic training or meditation, may produce verbal and observational changes, but do they also have the visceral or motoric effects that are hypothesized?

Which Dependent Measures?

Efforts to determine relaxation effects within and across behavior modalities raise questions about what measures to use as well as about the reliability and validity of these measures. Research establishing the reliability and validity of the BRS was described in Chapter 2, and applications described in Chapter 4 and the present chapter confirm its usefulness. However, the BRS is primarily a measure of motoric behavior, and measures of relaxation in other behavior modalities are needed. EMG activity is a widely accepted motoric measure of relaxation, but there are unanswered questions even with this. For example, multisite EMG recording rarely is employed, and little is known about patterns or generalization of muscle activity.

Recent development of verbal inventories suggests that this aspect of relaxation is increasing in interest (Crist, Rickard, Prentice-Dunn, & Barker, 1989; Smith, Amutio, Anderson, & Aria, 1996). Research on the reliability and validity of these or similar instruments, specifically their relationships to various training procedures and to other measures of relaxation, is a task that barely has begun. The BRS provides an established yardstick by which to compare other relaxation measurement devices.

Visceral and observational behavior is notoriously difficult to measure, as discussed in Chapter 2. Yet, these modalities play an important role in many problematic behaviors and in relaxation. Difficulty in measurement poses a challange to be taken up by researchers rather than avoided.

Questions of Clinical Significance

Process Measures and Treatment Outcome

Beyond the questions concerning which behaviors are affected by training is the matter of how these are related to treatment outcome. This raises issues about the measurement of treatment outcome such as validity of self- and other reports, use of concurrent and retrospective recording, physiological assessment, length of follow-up, and so forth that are beyond the scope of this book. The point here is that the relationship between proficiency in relaxation and treatment outcome is a valid research question. All members of the relaxation response class need to be entered into the equation. An initial step in this direction is exemplified by Wittrock, Blanchard, and McCoy (1988). In cases in which there is a hypothesized mechanism of action in a particular behavior domain such as muscle tension and headache or back pain, it is particularly important to assess changes in that domain. This can lend support to the formulation or can suggest that another mechanism needs to be investigated. Measures need to be obtained not only in the clinical setting but also in the trainee's home environment. Most treatment strategies assume that they are not simply providing "doses" of relaxation in the clinic but rather are teaching a skill that generalizes or is practiced in the trainee's everyday environment. This is another testable assumption. Improvements in electronic technology and miniaturization make portable EMG and visceral measures more available to clinical researchers, although these still are beyond the reach of practicing clinicians. The BRS and the Upright Relaxation Scale provide nonelectronic measures.

For example, BRT, like progressive relaxation and EMG biofeedback, is assumed to target changes in motoric behavior (muscle tension) that is measurable by the BRS. Changes in the BRS (and EMG levels) in the training and home environment can be related to changes in symptoms so as to test the treatment hypothesis. Observers can be trained in the client's home environment to score the BRS, as described in Chapter 4.

Clinical Effects of BRT

More clinical outcome studies of BRT are needed. Many stress and pain disorders are assumed to have muscle tension or asymmetry as a major component. For example, tension headache, temporomandibular joint disorder, and lower back pain lend themselves to treatment with BRT. Because of training ease and rapid learning by most individuals, BRT is proposed as a more efficient alternative to other motoric methods, namely progressive relaxation and EMG biofeedback. Or, in certain instances, it may be combined with them to form a more potent package.

In addition to motoric disorders, BRT can be applied with disorders in other domains. It can be combined beneficially with visceral procedures, such as thermal biofeedback or diaphragmatic breathing, for intervention with viscerally related problems such as asthma, panic attack, hypertension, and migraine. BRT may act in a synergistic fashion with observational procedures, such as guided imagery, for intervention with the observational component of disorders such as chronic pain or anxiety. Similarly, BRT may be augmented with verbal techniques such as autogenic training for problems in the verbal domain. All the suggested combinations of BRT with other methods, as described in an earlier section, await empirical validation.

Chapter 4 called attention to the need for treatment of arousal-related disorders in special populations. Early evidence indicates BRT is especially useful for persons with disabilities, and it has found a niche as a relaxation method for members of populations for whom relaxation training is uncommon. More research is needed to demonstrate not only that persons with disabilities can learn relaxation but also that it has a beneficial effect on their daily lives. More studies comparing and combining methods also are needed for persons in underserved populations.

Questions about treatment efficiency suggest a different sort of research design from that usually employed. A common procedure is to give a fixed number of treatment sessions and assess outcome in terms of average improvement on various measures in treatment and control groups. An alternative design is to set an improvement criterion, in terms of both proficiency in relaxed behaviors and symptom change, and to measure "trials to criterion" as a dependent variable. This can be accomplished in both single-subject and group research designs. This method more closely approximates clinical practice in which treatment continues until some level of satisfaction is reached (Poppen, 1983).

CONCLUSIONS

Research and clinical application of BRT have been exciting to the author and his students. To date, the evidence for its effectiveness and efficiency is promising. Similarly, the BRS has opened the door to issues in the assessment of relaxation. It is hoped that this book will serve as an antecedent for many others to join in the investigation.

Beyond the specific issues of BRT and the BRS as means of training and assessing relaxation, it is hoped that the conceptual framework presented here will generate a new look at this old topic. Presenting the various relaxation methods and theories from a behavioral viewpoint allows an empirical basis for comparison and evaluation research. Much hard work remains to be done before we can kick back and relax.

Appendix A:
Self-Report Rating Scale

1. Feeling deeply and completely relaxed throughout my entire body
2. Feeling very relaxed and calm
3. Feeling more relaxed than usual
4. Feeling relaxed as in my normal resting state
5. Feeling tension in some parts of my body
6. Feeling generally tense throughout my body
7. Feeling extremely tense and upset thoroughout my body

Appendix B:
Behavioral Relaxation Scale
Score Sheet

Client: _____ Date: _____   Time: _____   Provider(s): _____

Phase: BL Treatment Follow-up   Session number _____

BRT URT Biofeedback   Channels: 1. _____ 2. _____ 3. _____ 4. _____

Breathing Baseline: _____   Overall Assessment: (−) = Unrelaxed   (+) = Relaxed

	1		2		3		4		5		6		7		8		9		10		Total
		−	+	−	+	−	+	−	+	−	+	−	+	−	+	−	+	−	+	−	
Breathing		−	+	−	+	−	+	−	+	−	+	−	+	−	+	−	+	−	+	−	
Quiet		−	+	−	+	−	+	−	+	−	+	−	+	−	+	−	+	−	+	−	
Body		−	+	−	+	−	+	−	+	−	+	−	+	−	+	−	+	−	+	−	
Head		−	+	−	+	−	+	−	+	−	+	−	+	−	+	−	+	−	+	−	
Eyes		−	+	−	+	−	+	−	+	−	+	−	+	−	+	−	+	−	+	−	
Mouth		−	+	−	+	−	+	−	+	−	+	−	+	−	+	−	+	−	+	−	
Throat		−	+	−	+	−	+	−	+	−	+	−	+	−	+	−	+	−	+	−	
Shoulders		−	+	−	+	−	+	−	+	−	+	−	+	−	+	−	+	−	+	−	
Hands		−	+	−	+	−	+	−	+	−	+	−	+	−	+	−	+	−	+	−	
Feet		−	+	−	+	−	+	−	+	−	+	−	+	−	+	−	+	−	+	−	

Score Percentage

											Mean
EMG											
Thermal											

Pre-Observation Self-Rating:
Relaxation: 1 2 3 4 5 6 7
Pain: 0 1 2 3 4 5

Post-Observation Self-Rating:
Relaxation: 1 2 3 4 5 6 7
Pain: 0 1 2 3 4 5

NOTE: BL = baseline; BRT = Behavioral Relaxation Training; URT = Upright Relaxation Training.

Appendix C:
Written Criterion Tests
for Behavioral Relaxation
Scale Observers

Form A
1. List the 10 items scored on the BRS.
2. Which of the following are not considered to be relaxed?
    a. Chin sunk down on chest
    b. Shoulders sloped and even
    c. Feet crossed at the ankles
    d. Eyes open and focused on the middle distance
3. What is the optimal duration for a BRS observation period?
    a. 30 minutes
    b. 30 seconds
    c. 5 minutes
    d. 5 seconds

4. If a trainee clears her throat during an observation period, this could be scored as unrelaxed . . .
   a. Mouth
   b. Quiet
   c. Breathing
   d. Throat
5. How is percentage unrelaxed calculated?

Form B

1. List the 10 items scored on the BRS.
2. Which of the following are scored as relaxed behavior?
   a. Eyelids closed and smooth
   b. Lips closed with corners of the mouth downturned
   c. Hands folded in the lap
   d. Heels together and toes apart in a "V"
3. How long is breathing observed during each interval of the observation period?
   a. 30 seconds
   b. 30 minutes
   c. 5 seconds
   d. 5 minutes
4. If a trainee scratches his nose during an observation period, this would be scored as unrelaxed . . .
   a. Face
   b. Hands
   c. Head
   d. Body
5. How is percentage relaxed calculated?

Form C

1. List the 10 items scored on the BRS.
2. Relaxed breathing is defined as . . .
   a. The abdomen rises and falls while the shoulders remain stationary
   b. No movement of the chest, shoulders, or body
   c. Absence of interruptions such as coughing
   d. A rate slower than baseline

3. Each interval of the observation period consists of observing . . .
   a. Breathing for 20 seconds, other 9 items for 20 seconds, recording for 20 seconds
   b. 60 seconds observation for each item in succession
   c. Breathing for 30 seconds, other 9 items for 15 seconds, recording for 15 seconds
   d. All 10 items simultaneously for 60 seconds
4. If a trainee swallows during an observation period, this would be scored as unrelaxed . . .
   a. Mouth
   b. Throat
   c. Chest
   d. Body
5. How is reliability between two observers calculated?

NOTE: BRS = Behavioral Relaxation Scale.

Appendix D:
Behavioral Relaxation
Training Home Practice Form

Name: _____

Date	Time Start	Time End	Self-Rating	Difficult Items

Self-rating scale
7 = Extremely tense throughout my body
6 = Very tense in some areas of my body
5 = Somewhat tense in some areas of my body
4 = Neither tense nor relaxed (my usual resting state)
3 = Somewhat more relaxed than usual
2 = Generally relaxed in most of my body
1 = Deeply and completely relaxed throughout my body

References

Acosta, F. X., Yamamoto, J., & Wilcox, S. A. (1978). Application of electromyographic feedback to the relaxation training of schizophrenic, neurotic, and tension headache patients. *Journal of Consulting and Clinical Psychology, 46,* 383-384.

Agras, W. S., Taylor, C. B., & Kraemer, H. C. (1980). Relaxation training: 24-hour blood pressure reductions. *Archives of General Psychiatry, 37,* 859-863.

Arena, J. G., Blanchard, E. B., Andrasik, F., Cotch, P. A., & Myers, P. E. (1983). Reliability of psychophysiological assessment. *Behaviour Research and Therapy, 21,* 447-460.

Azrin, N. H. (1977). A strategy for applied research: Learning based but outcome oriented. *American Psychologist, 32,* 140-149.

Bacon, M., & Poppen, R. (1985). A behavioral analysis of diaphragmatic breathing and its effects on peripheral temperature. *Journal of Behavior Therapy and Experimental Psychiatry, 16,* 15-21.

Barber, T. X., & Hahn, K. W. (1963). Hypnotic induction and "relaxation": An experimental study. *Archives of General Psychiatry, 8,* 295-300.

Barkley, R. A. (1981). *Hyperactive children: A handbook for diagnosis and treatment.* New York: Guilford.

Benson, H. (1975). *The relaxation response.* New York: William Morrow.

Benson, H., Beary, J. F., & Carol, M. P. (1974). The relaxation response. *Psychiatry, 37,* 37-46.

Benson, H., & Friedman, R. (1985). A rebuttal to the conclusions of David S. Holmes' article, "Meditation and Somatic Arousal Reduction." *American Psychologist, 40,* 725-727.

Bernstein, D. A., & Borkovec, T. D. (1973). *Progressive relaxation training.* Champaign, IL: Research Press.

Blanchard, E. B. (1981). Behavioral assessment of psychophysiological disorders. In D. Barlow (Ed.), *Behavioral assessment of adult disorders* (pp. 239-269). New York: Guilford.

Blanchard, E. B., & Andrasik, F. (1985). *Management of chronic headaches.* New York: Pergamon.

Blanchard, E. B., McCoy, G. C., Musso, A., Gerardi, M. A., Pallmever, T. P., Gerardi, R. J., Cotch, P. A., Siracusa, K., & Andrasik, F. (1986). A controlled comparison of thermal biofeedback and relaxation training in the treatment of essential hypertension: I. Short-term and long-term outcome. *Behavior Therapy, 17,* 563-579.

Boice, R. (1983). Observational skills. *Psychological Bulletin, 93,* 3-29.

Booth-Kewley, S., & Friedman, H. S. (1987). Psychological predictors of heart disease: A quantitative review. *Psychological Bulletin, 101,* 343-362.

Borkovec, T. D., & Costello, E. (1993). Efficacy of applied relaxation and cognitive-behavioral therapy in the treatment of generalized anxiety disorder. *Journal of Consulting and Clinical Psychology, 61,* 611-619.

Boyer, B., & Poppen, R. (1995). Effects of abdominal and thoracic breathing upon multiple-site electromyography and peripheral skin temperature. *Perceptual and Motor Skills, 81,* 3-14.

Braith, J. A., McCullough, J. P., & Bush, J. P. (1988). Relaxation-induced anxiety in a subclinical sample of chronically anxious subjects. *Journal of Behavior Therapy and Experimental Psychiatry, 19,* 193-198.

Braunling-McMorrow, D. (1988). Behavioral rehabilitation. In P. Deutsch & K. Fralish (Eds.), *Innovations in head injury rehabilitation.* New York: Bender.

Brennan, R. (1996). *The Alexander technique manual.* Boston: Journey Editions.

Budzynski, T. H., & Stoyva, J. M. (1969). An instrument for producing deep muscle relaxation by means of analog information feedback. *Journal of Applied Behavior Analysis, 2,* 231-237.

Burgio, L. D., Whitman, T. L., & Johnson, M. R. (1980). A self-instructional package for increasing attending behavior in educable mentally retarded children. *Journal of Applied Behavior Analysis, 13,* 443-459.

Busenbark, K. L., Nash, J., Nash, S., Hupple, J. P., & Koller, W. C. (1981). Is essential tremor benign? *Neurology, 41,* 1982-1983.

Calamari, J. E., Geist, G. O., & Shahbazian, M. J. (1987). Evaluation of multiple component relaxation training with developmentally disabled persons. *Research in Developmental Disabilities, 8*, 55-70.

Carroll, D., Marzillier, J. S., & Merian, S. (1982). Psychophysiological arousal accompanying different types of arousing and relaxing imagery. *Psychophysiology, 19*, 75-82.

Cauthen, N. R., & Prymak, C. A. (1977). Meditation versus relaxation: An examination of the physiological effects of relaxation training and different levels of experience with transcendental meditation. *Journal of Consulting and Clinical Psychology, 45*, 496-497.

Chung, W. S. (1990). *Effects of relaxation and biofeedback training on tremor disorders.* Unpublished masters thesis, Southern Illinois University at Carbondale.

Chung, W., Poppen, R., & Lundervold, D. A. (1995). Behavioral relaxation training for tremor disorders in older adults. *Biofeedback and Self-Regulation, 20*, 123-135.

Cole, P. A., Pomerleau, C. S., & Harris, J. K. (1992). The effects of nonconcurrent and concurrent relaxation training on cardiovascular reactivity to a psychological stressor. *Journal of Behavioral Medicine, 15*, 407-414.

Cram, J. R., & Steger, J. C. (1983). EMG scanning in the diagnosis of chronic pain. *Biofeedback and Self-Regulation, 8*, 229-241.

Crist, D. A., & Rickard, H. C. (1993). A "fair" comparison of progressive and imaginal relaxation. *Perceptual and Motor Skills, 76*, 691-700.

Crist, D. A., Rickard, H. C., Prentice-Dunn, S., & Barker, H. R. (1989). The Relaxation Inventory: Self-report scales of relaxation training effects. *Journal of Personality Assessment, 53*, 716-726.

Dadds, M. R., Bovbjerg, D. H., Redd, W. H., & Cutmore, T. R. H. (1997). Imagery in human classical conditioning. *Psychological Bulletin, 122*, 89-103.

Davidson, R. J., & Schwartz, G. E. (1976). The psychobiology of relaxation and related states: A multi-process theory. In D. I. Mostofsky (Ed.), *Behavior control and modification of physiological activity* (pp. 399-442). Englewood Cliffs, NJ: Prentice Hall.

Dawson, M. E., Nuechterlein, K. H., Schell, A. M., Gitlin, M., & Ventura, J. (1994). Autonomic abnormalities in schizophrenia: State or trait indicators? *Archives of General Psychiatry, 51*, 813-824.

Donney, V. K. (1986). *Teaching parents to conduct behavioral relaxation training with their hyperactive children.* Unpublished masters thesis, Southern Illinois University at Carbondale.

Donney, V. K., & Poppen, R. (1989). Teaching parents to conduct behavioral relaxation training with their hyperactive children. *Journal of Behavior Therapy and Experimental Psychiatry, 20*, 319-325.

Elble, R. J., & Koller, W. C. (1990). *Tremor.* Baltimore, MD: Johns Hopkins University Press.

Fahn, S., Tolosa, E., & Marin, C. (1988). Clinical rating scale for tremor. In J. Jankovic & E. Tolosa (Eds.), *Parkinson's disease and movement disorders* (pp. 225-234). Baltimore, MD: Urban & Schwarzenberg.

Findley, L. J., & Capideo, R. (1984). *Movement disorders: Tremor.* London: Macmillan.

Fordyce, W. (1976). *Behavioral methods for chronic pain and illness.* St. Louis, MO: Mosby.

Foster, S. L., & Cone, J. D. (1986). Design and use of direct observation methods. In A. R. Ciminero, K. S. Calhoun, & H. E. Adams (Eds.), *Handbook of behavioral assessment* (2nd ed., pp. 253-324). New York: John Wiley.

Fried, R. (1993). The role of respiration in stress and stress control: Toward a theory of stress as a hypoxic phenomenon. In P. M. Lehrer & R. L. Woolfolk (Eds.), *Principles and practice of stress management* (2nd ed., pp. 301-331). New York: Guilford.

Gellhorn, E., & Loofbourrow, G. N. (1963). *Emotions and emotional disorders: A neurophysiological study.* New York: Harper & Row.

Goldiamond, I. (1974). Toward a constructional approach to social problems. *Behaviorism, 2,* 1-84.

Goyette, C. H., Conners, C. K., & Ulrich, R. F. (1978). Normative data on revised Conners parent and teacher rating scales. *Journal of Abnormal Child Psychology, 6,* 221-236.

Guercio, J., Chittum, R., & McMorrow, M. (1997). Self-management in the treatment of ataxia: A case study in reducing ataxic tremor through relaxation and biofeedback. *Brain Injury, 11,* 353-362.

Guercio, J., Ferguson, K., & McMorrow, M. (in press). Increasing functional communication abilities through neuromuscular feedback and relaxation training. *Brain Injury.*

Gutkin, A. J., Holborn, S. W., Walker, J. R., & Anderson, B. A. (1992). Treatment integrity of relaxation training for tension headaches. *Journal of Behavior Therapy and Experimental Psychiatry, 23,* 191-198.

Hanson, R. W., & Gerber, K. E. (1990). *Coping with chronic pain: A guide to patient self-management.* New York: Guilford.

Hartman, D. P., & Hall, R. V. (1976). The changing criterion design. *Journal of Applied Behavior Analysis, 9,* 527-532.

Harvey, J. R. (1979). The potential of relaxation training for the mentally retarded. *Mental Retardation, 17,* 71-76.

Heide, F. J., & Borkovec, P. D. (1983). Relaxation-induced anxiety: Paradoxical anxiety enhancement due to relaxation training. *Journal of Consulting and Clinical Psychology, 51,* 171-182.

Heide, F. J., & Borkovec, P. D. (1984). Relaxation-induced anxiety: Mechanisms and theoretical implications. *Behaviour Research and Therapy, 22,* 1-12.

Helfer, S. (1984). *Systematic desensitization with behavioral relaxation training: Assessment of cognitive, physiological, and behavioral response systems.* Unpublished masters thesis, Southern Illinois University at Carbondale.

Heller, T. (1982). The effects of involuntary residential relocation: A review. *American Journal of Community Psychology, 7,* 213-227.

Herson, M., & Barlow, D. H. (1976). *Single-case experimental designs: Strategies for behavior change.* New York: Pergamon.

Hess, W. R. (1957). *Functional organization of the diencephalon.* New York: Grune & Stratton.

Hillenberg, J. B., & Collins, F. L., Jr. (1982). A procedural analysis and review of relaxation training research. *Behaviour Research and Therapy, 20,* 251-260.

Hillenberg, J. B., & Collins, F. L., Jr. (1983). The importance of home practice for progressive relaxation training. *Behaviour Research and Therapy, 21,* 633-642.

Holmes, D. S. (1984). Meditation and somatic arousal reduction: A review of the experimental evidence. *American Psychologist, 39,* 1-10.

Horner, R. D., & Baer, D. M. (1978). Multiple-probe technique: A variation of the multiple baseline. *Journal of Applied Behavior Analysis, 11,* 189-196.

Jacobson, E. (1938). *Progressive relaxation.* Chicago: University of Chicago Press. (Originally published 1929)

Jankovic, J., Kurland, R. M., & Young, R. R. (1989, November 15). Managing the patient with tremor. *Patient Care,* pp. 33-38.

Javel, A. F., & Denholtz, M. S. (1975). Audible GSR feedback and systematic desensitization: A case report. *Behavior Therapy, 6,* 251-253.

Johnston, J. M., & Pennypacker, H. S. (1980). *Strategies and tactics of human behavioral research.* Hillsdale, NJ: Lawrence Erlbaum.

Keefe, F. J, , & Block, A. R. (1982). Development of an observation method for assessing pain behavior in chronic low back pain patients. *Behavior Therapy, 13,* 363-375.

King, N. J., & Montgomery, R. B. (1980). Biofeedback-induced control of human peripheral temperature: A critical review of the literature. *Psychological Bulletin, 88,* 738-751.

Koller, W. C. (1987). Essential tremor: A review. *Neurology, 37,* 1194-1197.

Krmpotich, J. D. (1986). *Behavioral relaxation in an upright chair: An electromyographic analysis.* Unpublished masters thesis, Southern Illinois University at Carbondale.

Lacey, J. I., & Lacey, B. C. (1958). Verification and extension of the principle of autonomic response stereotypy. *American Journal of Psychology, 71,* 50-73.

Lang, P. J. (1968). Fear reduction and fear behavior: Problems in treating a construct. In J. M. Shlien (Ed.), *Research in psychotherapy* (Vol. 3, pp. 90-103). Washington, DC: American Psychological Association.

Lang, P. J. (1977). Imagery in therapy: An information processing analysis of fear. *Behavior Therapy, 8,* 862-886.

Lang, P. J. (1979). A bio-informational theory of emotional imagery. *Psychophysiology, 16,* 495-512.

Lehrer, P. M., Carr, R., Sargunaraj, D., & Woolfolk, R. L. (1994). Stress management techniques: Are they all equivalent or do they have specific effects? *Biofeedback and Self-Regulation, 19,* 353-401.

Lehrer, P. M., Woolfolk, R. L., Rooney, A. J., McCann, B., & Carrington, P. (1983). Progressive relaxation and meditation: A study of psychophysiological and therapeutic differences between two techniques. *Behaviour Research and Therapy, 21,* 651-662.

Ley, R. (1988). Panic attacks during relaxation and relaxation-induced anxiety: A hyperventilation interpretation. *Journal of Behavior Therapy and Experimental Psychiatry, 19,* 253-259.

Liberman, R. P. (1986). Psychiatric rehabilitation of schizophrenia: Editor's introduction. *Schizophrenia Bulletin, 12,* 540-541.

Liberman, R. P., & Corrigan, P. W. (1993). Designing new psychosocial treatments for schizophrenia. *Psychiatry, 56,* 238-248.

Lindsay, W. R., & Baty, F. J. (1986a). Abbreviated progressive relaxation: Its use with adults who are mentally handicapped. *Mental Handicap, 14,* 123-126.

Lindsay, W. R., & Baty, F. J. (1986b). Behavioural relaxation training: Explorations with adults who are mentally handicapped. *Mental Handicap, 14,* 160-162.

Lindsay, W. R., & Baty, F. J. (1989). Group relaxation training with adults who are mentally handicapped. *Behavioural Psychotherapy, 17,* 43-51.

Lindsay, W. R., Baty, F. J., Michie, A. M., & Richardson, I. (1989). A comparison of anxiety treatments with adults who have moderate and severe mental retardation. *Research in Developmental Disabilities, 10,* 129-140.

Lindsay, W. R., Fee, M., Michie, A., & Heap, I. (1994). The effects of cue control relaxation on adults with severe mental retardation. *Research in Developmental Disabilities, 15,* 425-437.

Lindsay, W. R., & Morrison, F. M. (1996). The effects of behavioural relaxation on cognitive performance in adults with severe intellectual disabilities. *Journal of Intellectual Disability Research, 40,* 285-290.

Lishman, W. A. (1973). The psychiatric sequelae of head injury: A review. *Psychological Medicine, 3,* 304-318.

Lou, J. S., & Jankovic, J. (1991). Essential tremor: Clinical correlates in 350 patients. *Neurology, 41,* 234-238.

Ludwick-Rosenthal, R., & Neufeld, R. W. (1988). Stress management during noxious medical procedures: An evaluative review of outcome studies. *Psychological Bulletin, 104,* 326-342.

Luiselli, J. K. (1980). Relaxation training with the developmentally disabled: A reappraisal. *Behavior Research With Severe Developmental Disabilities, 1,* 191-213.

Luiselli, J. K., Marholin, K., II, Steinman, D. L., & Steinman, W. (1979). Assessing the effects of relaxation training. *Behavior Therapy, 10,* 663-668.

Lukoff, D., Liberman, R. P., Nuechterlein, K. H., & Ventura, J. (1986). Symptom monitoring in the rehabilitation of schizophrenic patients. *Schizophrenia Bulletin, 12,* 578-602.

Lundervold, D. A. (1986, December). The effects of behavioral relaxation and self-instruction training: A case study. *Rehabilitation Counseling Bulletin*, pp. 124-128.

Lundervold, D. A. (1995). *Effects of relaxation and biofeedback training on essential tremor and related disability.* Unpublished doctoral dissertation, Southern Illinois University at Carbondale.

Lundervold, D. A., & Poppen R. (1995). Biobehavioral rehabilitation of older adults with essential tremor. *The Gerontologist, 35,* 556-559.

Marks, I. M., & Mathews, A. M. (1979). Brief standard self-rating for phobic patients. *Behaviour Research and Therapy, 17,* 263-267.

Matson, J. L. (1985). Biosocial theory of psychopathology: A three by three factor model. *Applied Research in Mental Retardation, 6,* 199-227.

Mathews, A. M. (1971). Psychophysiological approaches to the investigation of desensitization and related procedures. *Psychological Bulletin, 76,* 73-91.

McCubbin, J. A., Wilson, J. F., Bruehl, S., Ibarra, P., Carlson, C. R., Norton, J. A., & Colclough, G. W. (1996). Relaxation training and opioid inhibition of blood pressure response to stress. *Journal of Consulting and Clinical Psychology, 64,* 593-601.

McGimpsey, B. A. (1982). *Behavioral relaxation training and assessment with developmentally disabled adults.* Unpublished masters thesis, Southern Illinois University at Carbondale.

McPhail, C. H., & Chamove, A. S. (1989). Relaxation reduces disruption in mentally handicapped adults. *Journal of Mental Deficiency Research, 33,* 399-406.

Meichenbaum, D., & Cameron, R. (1973). Training schizophrenics to talk to themselves. *Behavior Therapy, 4,* 515-534.

Michultka, D., Poppen, R., & Blanchard, E. B. (1988). Relaxation training as a treatment for chronic headaches in an individual having severe developmental disabilities. *Biofeedback and Self-Regulation, 13,* 257-266.

Miller, N. E. (1978). Biofeedback and visceral learning. *Annual Review of Psychology, 29,* 373-404.

Morse, R. H. (1983). Toward an eclectic stance in algology. *Seminars in Neurology, 3,* 355-358.

National Institutes of Health Technology Assessment Panel. (1996). Integration of behavioral and relaxation approaches into the treatment of chronic pain and insomnia. *Journal of the American Medical Association, 276,* 313-318.

Nigl, A., & Jackson, B. (1979). Electromyograph biofeedback as an adjunct to standard psychiatric treatment. *Journal of Clinical Psychiatry, 44,* 433-436.

Noe, S. R. (1997). *Behavioral relaxation training to reduce autonomic hyperarousal in individuals with schizophrenia.* Unpublished doctoral dissertation, Southern Illinois University at Carbondale.

Norton, G. R., & Johnson, W. E. (1983). A comparison of two relaxation procedures for reducing cognitive and somatic anxiety. *Journal of Behavior Therapy and Experimental Psychiatry, 14,* 209-214.

Norton, G. R., Rhodes, L., Hauch, J., & Kaprowy, E. A. (1985). Characteristics of subjects experiencing relaxation and relaxation-induced anxiety. *Journal of Behavior Therapy and Experimental Psychiatry, 16*, 211-216.

Norton, M., Holm, J. E., & McSherry, W. C., II. (1997). Behavioral assessment of relaxation: The validity of a behavioral rating scale. *Journal of Behavior Therapy and Experimental Psychiatry, 28*, 129-137.

O'Leary, K. D. (1980). Pills or skills for hyperactive children. *Journal of Applied Behavior Analysis, 13*, 191-204.

Olton, D. S., & Noonberg, A. R. (1980). *Biofeedback: Clinical applications in behavioral medicine.* Englewood Cliffs, NJ: Prentice Hall.

Ortega, D. F. (1978). Relaxation exercises with cerebral palsied adults showing spasticity. *Journal of Applied Behavior Analysis, 11*, 447-451.

Paul, G. L. (1969). Physiological effects of relaxation training and hypnotic suggestion. *Journal of Abnormal and Social Psychology, 74*, 425-437.

Peveler, R. C., & Johnston, D. W. (1986). Subjective and cognitive effects of relaxation. *Behaviour Research and Therapy, 24*, 413-419.

Pharr, O. M., & Coursey, R. D. (1989). The use and utility of EMG biofeedback with chronic schizophrenic patients. *Biofeedback and Self-Regulation, 14*, 229-245.

Poppen, R. (1983). Clinical practice and biofeedback research: Are the data really necessary? *The Behavior Therapist, 6*, 145-148.

Poppen, R. (1988). *Behavioral relaxation training and assessment.* New York: Pergamon.

Poppen, R. (1989). Some clinical implications of rule-governed behavior. In S. C. Hayes (Ed.), *Rule-governed behavior: Cognitions, contingencies, and instructional control* (pp. 325-357). New York: Plenum.

Poppen, R. (1995). *Key figures in psychotherapy: Joseph Wolpe.* London: Sage.

Poppen, R., Hanson, H., & Ip, S. V. (1988). Generalization of EMG biofeedback training. *Biofeedback and Self-Regulation, 13*, 235-243.

Poppen, R., & Maurer, J. (1982). Electromyographic analysis of relaxed postures. *Biofeedback and Self-Regulation, 7*, 491-498.

Qualls, P. J., & Sheehan, P. W. (1981). Electromyographic biofeedback as a relaxation training technique: A critical appraisal and reassessment. *Psychological Bulletin, 90*, 21-42.

Raymer, R. H., & Poppen, R. (1985). Behavioral relaxation training with hyperactive children. *Journal of Behavior Therapy and Experimental Psychiatry, 16*, 309-316.

Reinking, R. H., & Hutchings, D. (1981). Follow-up to: "Tension headaches: what form of therapy is most effective?" *Biofeedback and Self-Regulation, 6*, 57-62.

Reinking, R. H., & Kohl, M. L. (1975). Effects of various forms of relaxation training on physiological and self-report measures of relaxation. *Journal of Consulting and Clinical Psychology, 43*, 59-60.

Reiss, S. (1982). Psychopathology and mental retardation: A survey of a developmental disabilities mental health program. *Mental Retardation, 20*, 128-132.

Reiss, S., Levitan, G. W., & McNally, R. J. (1982). Emotionally disturbed mentally retarded people: An underserved population. *American Psychologist, 37*, 361-367.

Rickard, H. C., Collier, J. R., McCoy, A. D., Crist, D. A., & Weinberger, M. B. (1993). Relaxation training for psychiatric inpatients. *Psychological Reports, 72*, 1267-1274.

Rickard, H. C., Thrasher, K. A., & Elkins, P. D. (1984). Responses of persons who are mentally retarded to four components of relaxation instruction. *Mental Retardation, 22*, 248-252.

Russo, D. C., Bird, B. L., & Masek, B. J. (1980). Assessment issues in behavioral medicine. *Behavioral Assessment, 2*, 1-18.

Sapp, M. (1996). Three treatments for reducing the worry and emotionality components of test anxiety with undergraduate and graduate college students: Cognitive-behavioral hypnosis, relaxation therapy, and supportive counseling. *Journal of College Student Development, 37*, 79-87.

Sargent, J. D., Green, E. E., & Walters, E. D. (1973). Preliminary report on the use of autogenic feedback training in the treatment of migraine and tension headaches. *Psychosomatic Medicine, 35*, 129-135.

Schilling, D. J., & Poppen, R. (1983). Behavioral relaxation training and assessment. *Journal of Behavior Therapy and Experimental Psychiatry, 14*, 99-107.

Schultz, J. H., & Luthe, W. (1969). *Autogenic training* (Vol. 1). New York: Grune & Stratton.

Schwartz, J. H., Davidson, R. J., & Goleman, D. T. (1978). Patterning of cognitive and somatic processes in the self-regulation of anxiety: Effects of meditation versus exercise. *Psychosomatic Medicine, 40*, 321-328.

Sheikh, A. A. (1983). *Imagery: Current theory, research, and application.* New York: John Wiley.

Silver, B. V., & Blanchard, E. B. (1978). Biofeedback or relaxation training in the treatment of psychophysiologic disorders: Or, are the machines really necessary? *Journal of Behavioral Medicine, 1*, 217-239.

Skinner, B. F. (1953). *Science and human behavior.* New York: Macmillan.

Skinner, B. F. (1957). *Verbal behavior.* New York: Appleton-Century-Crofts.

Skinner, B. F. (1969). *Contingencies of reinforcement: A theoretical analysis.* New York: Appleton-Century-Crofts.

Skinner, B. F. (1974). *About behaviorism.* New York: Knopf.

Smith, J. C. (1989). *Relaxation dynamics: A cognitive-behavioral approach to relaxation.* Champaign, IL: Research Press.

Smith, J. C., Amutio, A., Anderson, J. P., & Aria, L.A. (1996). Relaxation: Mapping an uncharted world. *Biofeedback and Self-Regulation, 21*, 63-90.

BEHAVIORAL RELAXATION TRAINING AND ASSESSMENT

Southam, M. A., Agras, W. S., Taylor, C. B., & Kraemer, H. C. (1982). Relaxation training: Blood pressure lowering during the working day. *Archives of General Psychiatry, 39*, 715-717.

Spielberger, C. D. (1983). *State-Trait Anxiety Inventory.* Odessa, FL: Psychological Assessment Resources.

Stoyva, J. (1977). Self-regulation and the stress-related disorders: A perspective on biofeedback. In J. Kamiya, T. X. Barber, N. E. Miller, D. Shapiro, & J. Stoyva (Eds.), *Biofeedback and self-control 1976/1977* (pp. 3-21). Chicago: Aldine.

Surwit, R. S., & Keefe, F. (1978). Frontalis EMG feedback training: An electronic panacea? *Behavior Therapy, 9*, 779-792.

Tarler-Benlolo, L. (1978). The role of relaxation in biofeedback training: A critical review of the literature. *Psychological Bulletin, 85*, 727-755.

Taub, E., & Emurian, C. S. (1976). Feedback-aided self-regulation of skin temperature with a single feedback locus. *Biofeedback and Self-Regulation, 1*, 147-168.

Taylor, D. N., & Lee, C. T. (1991). Lack of correlation between frontalis electromyography and self-ratings of either frontalis tension or state anxiety. *Perceptual and Motor Skills, 72*, 1131-1134.

Taylor, S. L. (1983). *Behavioral relaxation training and assessment with traumatically brain-injured adults: Effects on motor performance.* Unpublished masters thesis, Southern Illinois University at Carbondale.

Wallace, R. K., Benson, H., & Wilson, A. F. (1971). A wakeful hypometabolic physiologic state. *Journal of Physiology, 221*, 795-799.

Weitzenhoffer, A. M., & Hilgard, E. R. (1962). *Stanford hypnotic susceptibility scales.* Palo Alto, CA: Consulting Psychologists Press.

Wells, A. (1990). Panic disorder in association with relaxation-induced anxiety: An attentional training approach to treatment. *Behavior Therapy, 21*, 273-280.

Werry, J., & Sprague, R., (1974). Methylphenidate in children: Effects of dosage. *Australian and New Zealand Journal of Psychiatry, 8*, 9-19.

Whalen, C., & Henker, B. (1976). Psychostimulants and children: A review and analysis. *Psychological Bulletin, 83*, 1113-1130.

Wittrock, D. A., Blanchard, E. B., & McCoy, G. C. (1988). Three studies on the relation of process to outcome in the treatment of essential hypertension. *Behaviour Research and Therapy, 26*, 53-66.

Wolpe, J. (1958). *Psychotherapy by reciprocal inhibition.* Stanford, CA: Stanford University Press.

Wolpe, J. (1969). *The practice of behavior therapy.* New York: Pergamon.

Wolpe, J. (1973). *The practice of behavior therapy* (2nd ed.). New York: Pergamon.

Wolpe, J., & Lang, P. J. (1964). A fear survey schedule for use in behavior therapy. *Behaviour Research and Therapy, 2*, 27-31.

Wolpe, J., & Lazarus, A. A. (1966). *Behavior therapy techniques: A guide to the treatment of neuroses.* Oxford, UK: Pergamon.

Wu, J., & Poppen, R. (1996, March). *Physiological and psychological effects of Tai Chi practice.* Poster presented at the meeting of the Association for Applied Psychophysiology and Biofeedback, Albuquerque, NM.

Yeaton, W. H., & Sechrest, L. (1981). Critical dimensions in the choice and maintenance of successful treatments: Strength, integrity, and effectiveness. *Journal of Consulting and Clinical Psychology, 49,* 156-167.

Zahara, D. (1983). *Behavioral relaxation training with traumatically head-injured adults.* Unpublished masters thesis, Southern Illinois University at Carbondale.

Author Index

Subject Index

About the Author

Roger Poppen is Professor and Coordinator of the Behavior Analysis and Therapy Program in the Rehabilitation Institute, Southern Illinois University at Carbondale. He received his Ph.D. in psychology from Stanford University in 1968. Since that time, he has conducted both basic and applied research in behavior analysis. His current interests are in the application of behavior analysis in stress, pain, and emotional disorders.